TRAVERSE
THEATRE

The Bush Theatre, in association with the Traverse Theatre, presents
the Traverse Theatre Company production of

Among Unbroken Hearts
by Henry Adam

cast in order of speaking

Ray	Adam Robertson
Neil	Mark Channon
Chaimig	Billy Riddoch
Amanda	Lesley Hart

director	John Tiffany
designer	Mark Leese
lighting designer	Natasha Chivers
music	Brian Docherty for scientific support dept.
voice coach	Ros Steen
Stage Manager	Gavin Harding
Deputy Stage Manager	Brendan Graham

**First performed at the Traverse Theatre
Friday 13 October 2000**

**First performed at the Bush Theatre
Wednesday 25 April 2001**

HENRY ADAM

Henry Adam is a Wick-born writer who has worked extensively in youth and community theatre in the Highlands and North East of Scotland. Recent plays include AN CLO MOR (Theatre Highland), THE ABATTOIR (Lemon Tree, Aberdeen), MILLENNIUM-ANGELS OF PARIS (His Majesty's Theatre, Aberdeen) and THE WIDOW for SHARP SHORTS (Traverse Theatre).

BIOGRAPHIES

Mark Channon (Neil): Theatre includes: 42ND STREET (Tour, Dominion); ANNIE GET YOUR GUN (Prince of Wales); A CHORUS LINE (Derby Playhouse); CRAZY FOR YOU (Prince Edward); SCROOGE (Dominion); SINGING IN THE RAIN (West Yorkshire Playhouse/National); DUMB WAITER (Covent Garden); PETER PAN, THE CRIPPLE OF INNISHMAN (National); TAP DOGS (UK & European tour). TV and film work includes: RAB C NESBITT, HARD MEN, created MONKHOUSE'S MEMORY MASTERS for BBC1, HIDDEN CAMERA SHOW (BBC); Enid Blyton's ENCHANTED LANDS. Mark is currently producing and appearing in the film THE CLEANERS.

Natasha Chivers (lighting designer): Recent work includes : CRAZY GARY'S MOBILE DISCO (Paines Plough); ORFEO (Opera North); A LISTENING HEAVEN (Royal Lyceum); PRISONER OF ZENDA (Watermill Theatre, Newbury); INTO OUR DREAMS (Almeida Site Specific Project); THE SALT GARDEN (Strathcona at The Maritime Museum, Greenwich); THE REEL OF THE HANGED MAN (Stellar Quines); TRISTAN AND ISOLDE (CPO,Tour/Royal Opera House); HYMNS, SELL OUT (Frantic Assembly).

Lesley Hart (Amanda): Trained: RSAMD. For the Traverse: SHETLAND SAGA. Final year productions include STAGS AND HENS and THE ART OF SUCCESS.

Mark Leese (designer): For the Traverse: SHETLAND SAGA, THE SPECULATOR, KILL THE OLD TORTURE THEIR YOUNG, KNIVES IN HENS, THE CHIC NERDS, GRETA, ANNA WEISS, WIDOWS, FAITH HEALER, THE HOPE SLIDE, BROTHERS OF THUNDER. Other recent work includes: FROGS (Royal National Theatre); THE PLAYBOY OF THE WESTERN WORLD, A FAMILY AFFAIR (Dundee Rep); MARTIN YESTERDAY (Royal Exchange, Manchester); A WEEKEND IN ENGLAND (Gateway, Chester); THE GREEKS (Theatre Babel); PARALLEL LINES (Theatre Cryptic); BORN GUILTY, THE WAR IN HEAVEN, THE GRAPES OF WRATH, THE SALT WOUND, ANTIGONE (7:84); ON GOLDEN POND (Royal Lyceum); BLACK COMEDY, PUBLIC EYE (Watford Palace). Film work includes: HOME (C4, BAFTA winner); HIDDEN, NIGHT SWIMMER, BILLIE AND ZORBA, SPITTING DISTANCE, GOLDEN WEDDING, CANDY FLOSS (BBC), GIRL IN THE LAY BY, GOOD DAY FOR THE BAD GUYS, RUBY (STV), CALIFORNIA SUNSHINE, HEART AND SOLE (C4). Mark is Design Associate at the Traverse.

Billy Riddoch (Chaimig): Theatre includes: THE CUT by Mike Cullen (Wiseguise); THREE SISTERS, MERCHANT OF VENICE, THE HYPOCONDRIAK (Royal Lyceum); MERLIN THE MAGNIFICENT, TARTUFFE, TOSHIE (Dundee Rep); Dame in MOTHER GOOSE (Citizens'). A member of John McGrath's 7:84 Theatre Company, appearing in over 20 productions for 7:84 and Wildcat, including: THE GAMES A BOGEY, BLOOD RED ROSES, LITTLE RED HEN, JOE'S DRUM, THE SILVER DARLINGS. TV work includes: Hammond in A TOUCH OF FROST; TAGGART, RAB C NESBIT, CLOUD HOWE, GLASGOW KISS and Lachlan in HAMISH MACBETH. Film includes: TRAINSPOTTING, SHALLOW GRAVE, DEATHWATCH. Radio work includes over 200 productions for the BBC including SUNSET SONG, MR BOLFRY and A CANTICLE FOR LIEBOVITCH.

Adam Robertson (Ray): Trained Drama Centre, London. Public performances at college include: Touchwood Junior in A CHASTE MAID IN CHEAPSIDE, Andri in ANDORRA, Orestes in ANDROMACHE. Theatre includes: Tantalus in THE KILLING FLOOR (Bridewell); Claudio in MUCH ADO ABOUT NOTHING (Royal Lyceum). Television work includes: PC Ron Jefferies in HARRY AND THE WRINKLIES (Series 1 & 2) (STV); BACK UP (BBC); THE ONE (GMTV); UNDER THE COVERS (Sky TV); Neil Morrison in TAGGART: THE MOVIE (STV). Film work includes: A MAN YOU DON'T MEET EVERY DAY (Channel 4).

Brian Docherty for scientific support dept. (music): collaborated with: Daddy's Favourite, Adventures In Stereo, Mount Vernon Arts Lab, This Mortal Coil, Vic Goddard. Remixed: Placebo, Shara Nelson & Alan Vega. Original music for Electrophobia (BBC), Clingfilm (Channel 4), 3 Shorts (Projectability), STROMA, OTHELLO (TAG); MACBETH (Awarehaus Theatre Company).
www.scientificsupportdept.com

Ros Steen (voice coach): Trained: RSAMD. Ros co-directed SOLEMN MASS FOR A FULL MOON IN SUMMER for the Traverse. As voice/dialect coach for the Traverse: THE TRESTLE AT POPE LICK CREEK; HERITAGE (1998 & 2001); SHETLAND SAGA, KING OF THE FIELDS, HIGHLAND SHORTS, FAMILY, KILL THE OLD TORTURE THEIR YOUNG, THE CHIC NERDS, GRETA, LAZYBED, KNIVES IN HENS, PASSING PLACES, BONDAGERS, ROAD TO NIRVANA, SHARP SHORTS, MARISOL, GRACE IN AMERICA, BROTHERS OF THUNDER. Other theatre includes: CASANOVA (SUSPECT CULTURE); SUNSET SONG (PRIME PRODUCTIONS); FUNHOUSE, OLEANNA, SUMMIT CONFERENCE, KRAPP'S LAST TAPE, THE DYING GAUL, CONVERSATION WITH A CUPBOARD MAN, EVA PERON, LONG DAY'S JOURNEY INTO NIGHT, (Citizens'); A.D. (Raindog); PLAYBOY OF THE WESTERN WORLD, A MIDSUMMER NIGHT'S DREAM (Dundee Rep); SEA URCHINS (Tron & Dundee Rep); HOME, TRANSATLANTIC, THE HANGING TREE, LAUNDRY and ENTERTAINING ANGELS (Lookout); ODYSSEUS THUMP (West Yorkshire Playhouse); BEUL NAM BREUG (Tosg Theatar Gaidhlig); TRAVELS WITH MY AUNT, THE PRICE (Brunton); TRAINSPOTTING (G & J Productions); HOW TO SAY GOODBYE, BABYCAKES (Clyde Unity); ABIGAIL'S PARTY (Perth Rep); LOVERS, PYGMALION, OUR COUNTRY'S GOOD (Royal Lyceum); SUNSET SONG (TAG). Film includes: GREGORY'S TWO GIRLS, STELLA DOES TRICKS, STAND AND DELIVER. Television includes: 2000 ACRES OF SKY, MONARCH OF THE GLEN, HAMISH MACBETH, LOOKING AFTER JOJO, ST ANTHONY'S DAY OFF, CHANGING STEP.

John Tiffany (director): Trained: Glasgow University. Literary Director at the Traverse since June 1997. For the Traverse: ABANDONMENT, KING OF THE FIELDS, THE JUJU GIRL, DANNY 306 + ME (4 EVER) (also Birmingham Rep), PERFECT DAYS (also Hampstead, Vaudeville and tour), GRETA, PASSING PLACES (also Citizens' and tour), SHARP SHORTS and STONES AND ASHES (co-director). Other theatre work includes: HIDE AND SEEK and BABY, EAT UP (LookOut); THE SUNSET SHIP (Young Vic); GRIMM TALES (Leicester Haymarket); EARTHQUAKE WEATHER (Starving Artists). Film includes: KARMIC MOTHERS (BBC Tartan Shorts) and GOLDEN WEDDING (BBC Two Lives).

**For generous help on Among Unbroken Hearts
the Traverse and the Bush thank:**

George Gunn and the all the actors who workshopped the play

North Edinburgh Drug Advice Centre; The Exchange Harm Reduction Team; The Frame Zone, Penicuik; Dr James Brown, Recruitment & Admissions, University of Glasgow; Boots the Chemist Earl Grey St, Edinburgh; Magnetic North Theatre Productions; Royal Lyceum Theatre; RSAMD; Scottish Opera; Eastern; BLF.

LEVER BROTHERS *for wardrobe care*

Sets, props and costumes for Among Unbroken Hearts
created by Traverse Workshops
(funded by the National Lottery

THE SCOTTISH ARTS COUNCIL
National Lottery Fund

production photography Kevin Low
print photography Euan Myles

THE BUSH THEATRE - THE WRITERS' THEATRE

One of the most experienced prospectors of raw talent in Europe
The Independent

Established in 1972 above the Bush pub in West London, the Bush Theatre quickly became an internationally renowned home of new writing. With hundreds of groundbreaking premieres and a string of awards to its credit, the Bush is devoted exclusively to the development, production and promotion of new plays.

Widely acclaimed as the seedbed for the best new playwrights, The Bush has launched the careers of such highly respected talents as Sharman MacDonald, Tony Kushner, Catherine Johnson, John Byrne, Victoria Wood, Lucy Gannon, Billy Roche, Jonathan Harvey and Conor McPherson.

The Bush regularly produces debut plays; the literary department receives, reads and reports on around 1,000 unsolicited scripts every year. Working closely with writers, the Bush issues five new commissions each year.

Many Bush plays have enjoyed national touring, transfers to the West End, Ireland, the USA and been developed for TV and film. Transfers have included DUET FOR ONE, WHEN I WAS A GIRL I USED TO SCREAM AND SHOUT, BEAUTIFUL THING and KILLER JOE, as well as adaptations of Billy Roche's WEXFORD TRILOGY (BBC2) and Jonathan Harvey's BEAUTIFUL THING (Film Four).

Touring in 2000/2001 has included HOWIE THE ROOKIE (UK tour then PS122, New York and The Magic Theatre, San Francisco) and RESIDENT ALIEN (Queer Up North Festival, Manchester and New York Theatre Workshop).

Open Doors, supported by the National Lottery Arts For Everyone Scheme, is a three year programme of writers' development including extra commissions, development weeks and workshops, residencies, training opportunities and writers' nights. The Bush Push is a scheme aimed specifically at encouraging young people to experience new drama. In addition, each year a young writer is appointed Writer in Residence at The Bush, receiving a commission supported by the Sheila Lemon legacy.

It remains, after 25 years, one of the liveliest centres of new writing. It also stays loyal to its discoveries. The West End may be starved of new work, but real drama flourishes at the Bush
Michael Billington, The Guardian

DEVELOPMENT

The Bush gratefully acknowledges core funding from London Arts and London Borough of Hammersmith and Fulham. In addition there are many individuals and companies whose generous support enables the theatre to nurture and develop new talent for the future. If you would like to find out more about becoming a supporter, please contact us on 020 7602 3703.

BUSH THEATRE
Shepherds Bush Green, London W12 8QD
Box office: 020 7610 4224
e-mail: info@bushtheatre.co.uk
www.bushtheatre.co.uk

LONDON ARTS

The Bush Theatre is a Registered Charity No. 270080

Coming Next...

6 June - 7 July
Blackbird
by Adam Rapp
Directed by Mike Bradwell
Designed by Lisa Lilywhite
Cast: Elizabeth Reaser and Paul Sparks

Blackbird presents us with a grimly compelling and ultimately doomed romance, shot through with moments of pure joy and tenderness that transcend the toxic lifestyles of two young lovers.

The Bush Theatre is proud to present the British debut of Adam Rapp, an outstanding new playwright, "a writer with a unique voice...a master of poetic realism" (The Boston Globe).

Box Office 020 7610 4224

TRAVERSE THEATRE

One of the most important theatres in Britain The Observer

Edinburgh's Traverse Theatre is Scotland's new writing theatre, with a 37 year record of excellence. With quality, award-winning productions and programming, the Traverse receives accolades at home and abroad from audiences and critics alike.

The Traverse has an unrivalled reputation for producing contemporary theatre of the highest quality, invention and energy, commissioning and supporting writers from Scotland and around the world and facilitating numerous script development workshops, rehearsed readings and public writing workshops. The Traverse aims to produce several major new theatre productions plus a Scottish touring production each year. It is unique in Scotland in its exclusive dedication to new writing, providing the infrastructure, professional support and expertise to ensure the development of a sustainable and relevant theatre culture for Scotland and the UK.

Traverse Theatre Company productions have been seen world wide including London, Toronto, Budapest and New York. Recent touring successes in Scotland include the original touring production of AMONG UNBROKEN HEARTS, PERFECT DAYS by Liz Lochhead, PASSING PLACES by Stephen Greenhorn, HIGHLAND SHORTS, HERITAGE by Nicola McCartney and LAZYBED by Iain Crichton Smith. PERFECT DAYS also played the Vaudeville Theatre in London's West End in 1999. In 2000 the Traverse co-produced Michel Tremblay's SOLEMN MASS FOR A FULL MOON IN SUMMER with London's Barbican Centre, with performances in both Edinburgh and London, and two world permieres as part of the Edinburgh Festival Fringe: SHETLAND SAGA by Sue Glover and ABANDONMENT by Kate Atkinson.

The Traverse can be relied upon to produce more good-quality new plays than any other Fringe venue
Daily Telegraph

During the Edinburgh Festival the Traverse is one of the most important venues with world class premieres playing daily in the two theatre spaces. The Traverse regularly wins awards at the Edinburgh Festival Fringe, including recent Scotsman Fringe Firsts for Traverse productions KILL THE OLD TORTURE THEIR YOUNG by David Harrower and PERFECT DAYS by Liz Lochhead.

An essential element of the Traverse Company's activities takes place within the educational sector, concentrating on the process of playwriting for young people. The Traverse flagship education project CLASS ACT offers young people in schools the opportunity to work with theatre professionals and see their work performed on the Traverse stage. In addition the Traverse runs Young Writers groups for 15 - 25 year olds and Shining Souls, a writers group for people aged 55+. All groups are led by professional playwrights.

SPONSORSHIP

Sponsorship income enables the Traverse to commission and produce new plays and offer audiences a diverse and exciting programme of events throughout the year.

We would like to thank the following companies for their support throughout the year:

CORPORATE ASSOCIATE SCHEME

LEVEL ONE
Sunday Herald
Balfour Beatty
Scottish Life the PENSION company
United Distillers & Vintners
Amanda Howard Associates

 **BANK OF SCOTLAND**

LEVEL TWO
Laurence Smith -
Wine Merchants
Willis Corroon Scotland Ltd
Wired Nomad

LEVEL THREE
Alistir Tait FGA
Antiques & Fine Jewellery
Nicholas Groves Raines -
Architects
KPMG
Scottish Post Office Board

 Scotland

With thanks to
Navy Blue Design, print designers for the Traverse,
and Stewarts Colour Print
Arts & Business for management and mentoring services
Purchase of the Traverse Box Office, computer network and technical and training equipment has been made possible with money from
The Scottish Arts Council National Lottery Fund.

THE SCOTTISH ARTS COUNCIL
National Lottery Fund

The Traverse Theatre's work would not be possible without the support of

 THE SCOTTISH ARTS COUNCIL

 •EDINBVRGH•
THE CITY OF EDINBURGH COUNCIL

The Traverse receives financial assistance for its educational and development work from

John Lewis Partnership, Peggy Ramsay Foundation, Binks Trust, The Yapp Charitable Trusts, The Bulldog Prinsep Theatrical Trust, Calouste Gulbenkian Foundation, Gannochy Trust, The Garfield Weston Foundation, The Paul Hamlyn Foundation, JSP Pollitzer Charitable Trust, The Hope Trust, Steel Trust, Craignish Trust, Esmee Fairbairn Trust, Lindsay's Charitable Trust, Tay Charitable Trust

Charity No. SC002368

ix

TRAVERSE THEATRE - THE COMPANY

AMONG UNBROKEN HEARTS

Henry Adam

For Jo

Characters

RAY

NEIL

AMANDA

CHAIMIG

ACT ONE

Scene One

A farmhouse in the far north of Scotland. The atmosphere is of age and dust and cobwebs, of lives that have passed. There is a door leading to a kitchen and from that direction two young men, RAY and NEIL, enter. They are carrying travel bags, which they drop near the door as they acclimatise themselves to their new surroundings. One of the men – NEIL – tries a light switch. Nothing happens.

NEIL. No power.

RAY. Look above e door. Probably e mains.

> NEIL *goes back into the kitchen.* RAY *moves inside, looking around the room as if remembering it from a dream. His fingers play with the dust. He picks up a framed photograph from a sideboard, wipes it clean. He is subdued. Everything he touches he touches with reverence.*

NEIL (*voice-off*). Yeah, I've got it. Zat it?

> RAY *switches on a lamp.*

RAY (*to himself*). I sing the hydro-electric.

NEIL. What?

RAY. Nothing, just a joke. Is thur water?

NEIL. Water's okay. Plastic kettle too. Know where ye are wi' plastic. (*Looking around.*) Jesus. (*Shakes head.*) Home sweet home.

RAY. Yeah. Home sweet home.

NEIL (*seeing dust, shakes head*). Jeez.

RAY. Ma faither lived here. Right back at the start o his life. When they came back fie Australia they moved in here. Wi' ma granny's granny.

NEIL. What were they doing in Australia?

RAY. Ma granny went til make her fortune. She made a baby instead.

NEIL. Ma granny wiz a servant. Do ye believe at? A fucking servant.

RAY. Yeah. Mine too. Both of them. They had masters. They worked for masters.

NEIL. Zat how she got pregnant? Playin masters an servants.

RAY. Fuck knows. When ma faither died a hed til get e death certificate. A went doon an e registrar, e lassie Cowie, she says – what about yur grandfaither? Is he still alive? A hed no idea, never even crossed ma mind. So a asked ma mither. Dinna ask me, she says, ask yur granny. So a did. Know what she said? E last time a saw at bastard wiz Perth, Australia 1927.

NEIL. So he could still be alive?

RAY. Sure. E ither wan too. Efter at I got curious. I asked ma mither where her faither wiz buried. Ye've got t' be dead t' be buried, at's what she said. Wisna til a loast ma faither it a found oot a hed two grandfaithers. At' s ma history, ye know? At's who I am.

NEIL. Nobody has roots any more Ray. It was on the news. Did nobody tell ye?

RAY. Is that the new dictate?

NEIL. Yeah, welcome to the marketplace. You're an individual now boy, a free man in a free land. You thought you had no future, fact is you've got no past. Nobody cares who you are anymore. They just want to know what you want to buy.

RAY. Suits me.

NEIL. Yeah?

RAY. Yeah.

NEIL. What's e book?

>RAY *has picked up an old book that was lying around. He hands it now to* NEIL.

RAY. It's a school prize or something. Presented to David Sinclair, July 1932.

NEIL. Zat your dad?

RAY. Yeah. Perfect attendance 1931/32. Stubborn little bastard.

>RAY *continues to reacquaint himself with the room while* NEIL *reads.*

NEIL. 'All children, except one, grow up. They soon know that they will grow up, and the way Wendy knew was this. One day when she was two years old she was playing in a garden, and she plucked another flower and ran with it to her mother. I suppose she must have looked rather delightful, for Mrs Darling put her hand to her heart and cried – 'Oh why can't you remain like this forever!' This was all that passed between them on the subject, but henceforth Wendy knew that she must grow up. You always know after you are two. Two is the beginning of the end'. Jesus. I thought I was a fucking pessimist.

RAY. D'ye want some tea?

NEIL. All the tea in China.

RAY. All the tea in china cups.

>RAY *goes into the backpacks to get the tea. When he gets it he will go into the kitchen to put on the kettle, then return to hover in the doorway.*

NEIL. It'll be okay here, eh? Okay for a couple o days. Couple o days withoot every cunt in toon knockin on your door.

RAY. Yeah. It'll be okay.

NEIL. Ye need it sometimes, do ye noh? A break. It was getting pretty hairy back ere for a while. A hed at bastard

Duguid on my back again last week. Did I tell ye? Says I'm rippin him off. He gets me up against e wall, yeah, so I push him off an gie him a smack. He goes in his back pocket. Comes oot wi' a spoon. 'What ye gonna do wi' at?' I said. 'Scoop me?' (*Shakes head, amused by himself.*) Scoop me?

RAY. Duguid's a prick.

NEIL. Yeah, I know. They all are.

NEIL *wanders restlessly, looking out the window/door.*

NEIL. So this is the country eh? Fucking country. Never really been in the country before. Thought it would be different, you know? Thought there'd be more coos or something.

RAY. Welcome to County Hell.

NEIL. What?

RAY. Just what we used to call it. Me and Christie. County Hell. East Jesusville, County Hell, United States of Shit. Cool address, eh?

NEIL. Looks okay to me.

RAY. Yeah, well. All ye city boys are chaist teuchters at heart. Should see it in winter. Nothing between us an e arctic. Fucking dark most o e time. Fucking rains e rest. Used to be able to read by e light o e shotgun blasts. Poor sun starved bastards blowing their heads off rather than endure another day.

NEIL. Why bother coming back if ye hate it so much?

RAY (*shrugs*). Why do Lemmings jump off cliffs?

NEIL. I've got a theory aboot at.

RAY. I'll bet ye do.

RAY *goes back to the kitchen.*

NEIL. Goes back to the time before the continental shift. They're heading for their old breeding grounds. It's wired into their blood. Hard drive. Couldna stop even if they wanted to. Just keep on going. (*Illustrates the trajectory of a lemming.*)

RAY *returns with the tea.*

RAY. I wrote some poems about this place. You should read them sometime.

RAY *takes a cigarette packet out of his pocket and empties its contents – everything needed to prepare a shot of heroin – onto the table, and proceeds to cook up a hit at a leisurely pace.*

NEIL. Remember Beth? She had this poem she wrote. She kept it in her drawer wi' all her socks and stuff. A love poem. It was good. Lek Shakespeare or something. It rhymed. I used to think it was really sweet, you know, the way she kept it hidden lek at, lek it was something precious or something, an e way she showed it to you, lek she was sharing something, more than just . . . (*Takes out own works, shrugs.*) you know.

RAY. Yeah. She showed it to me too.

NEIL. Yeah?

RAY. She showed it to everybody before they fucked her. At least I think she did. It was like some weird kind of foreplay or something. It was good though. Made you forget for a few minutes she was mad.

NEIL. She wiz mad though.

RAY. She was 100 fucking pain.

NEIL. Christ, I remember her once jumping up and down on the mattress like it was a fucking trampoline or something, just wearing a pair o tights, black tights. Her tits were flopping about all over the place. She was chanting 'I'm crazy, crazy, crazy!' and I was thinking, Noh, you're noh crazy you're just really, really sad. Your boyfriend's dead and they've taken your kids and you're sad, sad, sad, and it only feels like crazy because nobody's ever been as sad as you before. She was crazy though. It was only the largactyl that was holding her together. It's really weird screwing somebody who's on largactyl. Like they're all tied up an ye canna see e ropes. Invisible chains. Lek in a fairy tale or something.

RAY. She said to me once – 'I really like you, you're just like Eddie', an I said – 'What? Dead?'

NEIL. You are like Eddie. Same face.

RAY. Guess he was a pretty good-looking guy then.

NEIL. Won the prettiest corpse competition two years runnin. Everybody down at the graveyard was so proud.

RAY. Eddie was a prick.

NEIL. Thought ye said ye didna ken him?

RAY. He died. It's only pricks who die.

NEIL. John. Donald. George.

RAY. I know their names.

RAY *has gotten up from the table during this exchange. He moves away, controlling his agitation. NEIL watches him. NEIL goes to the table and starts cooking up a hit of his own. RAY broods by the window/door.*

NEIL. I had a guy o.d. on me once, did I tell ye? Hit him up wi' salt. Gave him the kiss o life. I was pounding on his chest lek a demented ape when Christie walks in. This guy's dead on the kitchen floor and Christie goes – 'What time is it? I want to get some Lemonade before e chip shop shuts.' Probably could've saved him if it wizna for at. Couldna blow in his mouth for laughing.

RAY (*bitterly*). Yeah well, at's Christie for ye.

NEIL. Did he ever come out here?

RAY. Nah. Christie hated e country.

NEIL *glances up at* RAY, *noticing him growing more distant.*

NEIL. I always fancied it. When I was a kid. Used to have all these fantasies, ye know? Just take off. Sleep in haystacks. Too much Enid Blyton, eh? Closest I ever got was Seaton Park. So how long did ye live here?

RAY. A lived in e toon. Weeck. Next door to Christie. (*Gestures towards town with head.*) Chaist used to come here in e summers. School holidays, ye know?

NEIL. Summers, eh? Were they blissfully idyllic?

RAY. Yeah.

NEIL. Sorta 'As I was green and carefree'.

RAY. Yeah.

NEIL. Lek 'Little House on the Prairie'.

RAY. More lek 'E Waltons'. Noh, 'Doctor Finlay'. 'Och, it's yourself Janet'.

NEIL *laughs.* RAY *notices a picture of himself and an old man. He picks it up. He takes it across to* NEIL.

RAY. Look. At's me. Five years old.

NEIL. Cute. Who's e guy?

RAY. Chaimig. He used to work here, helpin oot ma granny. Gettin under her feet she'd call it. He used til take me wi' him when he went oot. Up til e lambs an stuff. It was good. Taught me a lot.

NEIL. A father figure?

RAY. Yeah well, at's what all us girls are looking for. Hevna seen him in years.

NEIL. Still alive?

RAY. Yeah. Far as a know. I'll maybe go up an see him. While I'm here.

RAY *goes back to the table and continues cooking up. The two concentrate on what they are doing.* RAY *glances up.*

RAY. D'ye ever think aboot it, Neil?

NEIL. What?

RAY. Dying?

NEIL (*smiling, unsettled by the question*). Noh. Who's gonna die?

RAY. Yeah. Who's gonna die?

> RAY *shivers.* NEIL *straps a belt around his arm and edges the needle towards his vein.*

Scene Two

Later that night. The kitchen area of another rural home. A teenage girl, AMANDA, sits at the table. She has an unopened letter in her hand. She seems to be contemplating opening it, dreading it at the same time. An old man, CHAIMIG, enters. He finds his way around the kitchen with the help of a white stick. He is trying to make a cup of coffee. He spills it and lashes out in frustration.

CHAIMIG. Dammitalltilhell!

AMANDA. Ye okay, grandad?

CHAIMIG. A scailt iss damned coffee.

AMANDA. Go through an sit, a'll make ye anither ine.

CHAIMIG. Christ Amanda, a can make a cup o coffee, a'm noh a bloody bairn.

AMANDA. Noh, a know yur noh. Chaist let me do it, eh. Save ye missin yur programme.

> AMANDA *takes over, wiping up the mess* CHAIMIG *has made. As she does her eyes glance out through the window, and something surprises her.*

AMANDA. At's funny.

CHAIMIG. Fit is?

AMANDA. Did ye hear anything aboot anybody movin in til Sadie's?

CHAIMIG. Sadie's?

AMANDA. Aye. Thurs smok comin fie her chimney.

CHAIMIG. Noh, a never heard a word. Boot then fa'd tell me. Yur e ine wi'e lugs it wid make an elephant envy.

AMANDA. A never heard anything.

CHAIMIG. An here's me thinkin it niything got done aroond here withoot yur say so.

AMANDA. Yur noh funny.

CHAIMIG. Am a wearin a riyd nose? Anyway, id's aboot time somebody wiz takin id on. An empty hoose is noh use til anybody. A micht even go so far as til say id' s an abomination, bearin in mind e times wur livin through.

AMANDA. It'll be funny, hevin somebody else so close efter all iss time.

CHAIMIG. Aye, id'll noh be e same. Still. Time marches on. (*Getting to feet.*) Are ye takin at through?

AMANDA. Aye.

CHAIMIG. Weel, dinna forget ma biscuit.

CHAIMIG *exits.* AMANDA *goes to take* CHAIMIG*'s coffee through but is interrupted by a knock to the door.*

AMANDA. Chaist a meenid.

Another knock.

AMANDA. Aye. A'm comin.

She opens the door to RAY.

RAY (*seeing* AMANDA *and smiling*). Hey, Amanda.

AMANDA. Ray? Jesus.

RAY. Long time no see, eh?

AMANDA. Say at again. God, Ray. Fit ye doin here?

RAY. I'm chaist back for a few days. Thought I'd come up an see Chaimig while I'm here. Is he in?

AMANDA. Aye, he's chaist through watchin e telly.

RAY. Hez he got ye runnin aroond efter him now?

AMANDA. Aye, something lek at.

RAY. Christ, last time a saw ye ye were iss high. (*Indicates height.*)

AMANDA. A dinna think so. A micht've been yowng boot a wiz never at small.

RAY. I should know. Babysat for ye often enough.

AMANDA. God, at wiz a long time ago. Here, wait, a'll . . .

CHAIMIG (*voice-off*). Amanda? Fa's at yur yakkin til now? If id's at Jock Gow tell him yur mither'll be in til see him first o e week.

AMANDA. Noh, it's . . . Grandad, ye've got a visitor.

CHAIMIG. A visitor? Fa's visitin me? Marion? Is at ye lassie?

RAY. Come through an look. Thur'll mibbe be a dram waitin for ye if ye do.

CHAIMIG. Here, a ken at voice. Fa's at now? (*He appears in doorway.*) Raymond? Is at ye boy?

RAY *sees* CHAIMIG *is blind. His shock is visible. He looks to* AMANDA.

RAY. Aye . . . Aye, it's me . . .

CHAIMIG. Comere then. A willna bite. Let me take a look at ye. (*He puts his hand to* RAY'*s face.*) Ye've loast weight loon. Are they noh feedin ye?

RAY. Aye, they're feedin me. They're feedin me fine. Christ Chaimig . . . fit happened?

CHAIMIG. Fit happened? Niything happened. A'm chaist owld. E bugger catches up wi' all o us in e end.

AMANDA. Grandad's blind Ray.

CHAIMIG. Christ Amanda, div ye noh think he can see at? Are thur twa blin men in iss kitchen?

AMANDA. A wiz chaist sayin.

CHAIMIG. Well dinna chaist say! Christ, wan thing a canna stan – fowk statin e damned obvious. Anyway . . . far's iss dram ye were shoutin aboot? Or hev ye dragged me through here under false pretenses?

RAY. Noh, here . . . I took up a half bottle.

CHAIMIG. A half bottle? Christ min, a wiz expectin a case o e McAllan e next time ye showed yur fiyce.

RAY. I'm a poor man Chaimig. A half bottle's all a could afford.

CHAIMIG. Get rich then! Wur livin through fat years, or so at feels on e telly keep tellin us. Could ye noh hev done fit at mannie Tebbit did an get on yur bike. On yur bike. Wiz at noh a terrible thing til say. Millions o men oot o work an he tells them til get on thur bikes.

RAY. Aye, an then they kick up a stink aboot e number o bicycles bein stolen.

CHAIMIG. Oh aye, id's in e bible ye ken. Thou shalt not covet thy neighbour's bicycle.

AMANDA. A think yull find at's 'Ass', grandad.

CHAIMIG. I beg your pardon, Miss Donaldson? Did ye hev something til contribute?

AMANDA. 'Ass'. 'Thou shalt not covet thy neighbour's ass'.

CHAIMIG. An tell me Miss Fancypants, if bicycles hed been invented back then div ye think it still wid've been Ass?

AMANDA. A donno grandad. A suppose it wid depend on
how cute an ass it wiz.

CHAIMIG. What did she say? What did she say? Christ. As
bad as her mither at ine. A tell ye, Raymond, a've bred a
dynasty o cheeky wimmen. A dynasty. A dinna ken far they
get thur towngs fie, noh fie ma side o e femly at's for sure.
A come fie circumspect stock – tight-lipped, stiff-backed,
God-fearin Presbyterian stock. A dinna ken fit happened,
thur must've been a tink involved in e equation some pliyce
doon e line.

RAY. Ye canna bliyme e tinks for everything.

CHAIMIG. Christ Raymond, ye've got til bliyme somebody
for at lot. E implications o anything else are too terrible til
countenance.

AMANDA. Ye love us really.

CHAIMIG. Oh, a love ye, boot thurs a difference atween love
and approval. Yull ken at for yursel though, a wid think.

RAY. Christ . . . Wiz thur niything they could do Chamig?
Some operation or something . . .?

CHAIMIG. Do? Christ Raymond, a'm seventy four year owld.
Fit div ye think a'm goin til see now it a hevna seen
already?

RAY. Aye. It's chaist a shock. E last time a saw ye ye could
still . . .

CHAIMIG. See? Christ Raymond, a can still see, a chaist see
different things, at's all . . . Different things. Ye've hed
troubles yursel a wiz hearin?

RAY. Me?

CHAIMIG. Aye. Did somebody noh say it yur freend died, fit
wis his niym again?

AMANDA. Christie.

CHAIMIG. Aye, e Sutherland loon.

RAY. Ye heard aboot at?

CHAIMIG. Aye. Id wiz in e piyper they were sayin.

AMANDA. He drooned, did he noh?

RAY. Aye. He drooned.

CHAIMIG. Ma brither drooned, Christ – sixty year ago now. Noh a diyth a ever fancied muckle. He widna've been muckle owlder than ye, wid he, e Sutherland loon?

RAY. Younger. Twenty two.

CHAIMIG. Aye. Twenty two's noh muckle, is it? At's noh age at all.

RAY. Too young to die at's for sure.

AMANDA. So how did ye get up Ray? Did ye take e bus?

RAY. The bus? Noh, we hitched.

CHAIMIG. Hitched? Christ, ye are poor. Uch weel, it'll be iysier for ye when id comes til gettin in til heaven, niyn o at squeezin camels through needles an fit hev ye. Still, a'd raither be rich an take ma chances. Are they hevin a service for e Sutherland loon? Is at fit yur back for?

RAY. A donno. A chaist fancied a break. A hevna been back since my granny died.

CHAIMIG. Noh. Ye werena at e funeral were ye?

RAY. Noh, a wiz awiy, a never heard til it wiz too late.

CHAIMIG. Aye, at's too bad. She wid've wanted ye ere.

RAY. Aye . . . I know . . .

AMANDA. Yur here now.

CHAIMIG. Aye. Yur here now.

AMANDA. Come on ye, do ye want iss drink or noh?

CHAIMIG. Aye, why noh? Even if it's noh e McAllan.

RAY. A'll try and do better e next time.

AMANDA. A widna worry aboot it Ray. He canna tell e difference anyway.

CHAIMIG. I take offence at at, Miss Donaldson.

AMANDA. At's noh lek ye.

CHAIMIG. A'll hev ye ken a'm a connoisseur o whisky. Or at least a used til be. Fuckin doctors put a stop til at.

AMANDA. Grandad!

CHAIMIG. Well then, fit div ye expect . . . ye'd think a'd drunk masel blin til listen til them.

AMANDA. Ye probably did.

CHAIMIG. Christ, whisky never hurt anybody. Id's weel known for it's restorative qualities.

AMANDA. It'll take more than a half bottle til restore ye.

CHAIMIG. Christ, a'll restore ye. Ye hear fit a've got til pit up wi'?

RAY. Aye, a hear.

AMANDA. Are ye hom a while Ray?

RAY. A donno. Couple o days maybe.

CHAIMIG. Doon at Sadie's?

RAY. Aye.

AMANDA. At's e smok we saw. – We thocht they'd sold id.

RAY. Noh, it' s mine now.

CHAIMIG. She left id til ye, did she? Weel, at's something. Here now. Wid ye do something for me. Raymond, seein as yur here? Wid ye come up some efternoon an take a walk wi' me. Iss ine ken, she'll take me doon til e bottom o e road an back. Thinks a'll trip ower an hurt masel. But ye . . . yu'll take a walk wi' me?

RAY. Aye sure. E way ye walked wi' me.

CHAIMIG. By God! At wis a while ago now.

RAY. Aye, it seems it, eh?

CHAIMIG. By god, at wiz a while ago. Well . . . here's til us.

RAY. Aye, fa's lek us?

CHAIMIG. Gae few, gae few.

They drink. Silence.

RAY. I'd better be makin a move.

CHAIMIG. Yur goin?

RAY. Aye. A've left somebody doon at e hoose. He'll be wonderin far a am.

CHAIMIG. Christ, ye chaist got here.

RAY. Aye. A wiz chaist passin . . . thought a'd see if ye were in.

CHAIMIG. Christ, hev anither dram. Amanda! Gie e man a dram.

RAY. Noh, it's okay. A should go.

CHAIMIG. Ye've hardly heard wir news yet.

RAY. A wiz chaist passin . . .

CHAIMIG. Christ Amanda . . . poor e man a drink.

AMANDA. He's got til go grandad.

CHAIMIG. Christ laskie, will ye noh do fit yur telt. Christ, a'll do it masel! Here, sit doon now. Sit!

CHAIMIG *has gotten excited. He rises too quickly then falls back down clutching his chest/ breathing heavily.*

AMANDA. Grandad!

CHAIMIG. A'm fine. Chaist let me catch ma briyth!

AMANDA. Yur noh fine. Comere now, dinna . . .

CHAIMIG. Dinna fuss! A'm . . . a'm . . . God, a'm fine.

AMANDA. A'm puttin ye til yur bed.

CHAIMIG. Christ Amanda, a'm noh a bairn.

AMANDA. A know, a know . . . chaist for a meenid . . . chaist
til ye get yur briyth back.

CHAIMIG. Raymond . . .

RAY. Aye . . . I'm here.

AMANDA. Dinna worry aboot Ray. He'll come up an see ye
tomorrow, will ye noh?

CHAIMIG. Raymond . . .?

RAY. Aye. It's okay. I'll come up tomorrow. I'll come up
tomorrow and we'll go for at walk.

CHAIMIG. A walk? Christ Amanda . . . div ye think he's tryin
til kill me?

AMANDA. Aye, we're all tryin til kill ye.

CHAIMIG. Dammit, a thocht as much.

> CHAIMIG *tries to laugh, but is caught up in wheezing.*
> AMANDA *leads him away.* RAY *watches helplessly. He
> falls back into his seat.* AMANDA *returns, sits. She takes
> one of* CHAIMIG's *Woodbines and lights it.*

RAY. Will he be all right?

AMANDA. Yeah. He chaist got excited. He'll be fine.

RAY. Christ. How long's he been lek at?

AMANDA. Aboot a year now. It comes and goes. He's noh
used til visitors. At's all id is.

RAY. Nobody comes?

AMANDA. They're all gone now. A think Sadie wiz e last.

RAY (*shaking head*). I shouldna hev come.

AMANDA. Dinna be silly. He's always lek'd ye. He still goes on aboot ye – when ye were a bairn an at; how yull be a great man some day.

RAY. Me?

AMANDA. Aye. He says yur a poet, is at right?

RAY. A poet? Noh. Noh really. Look, I'd better go. Tell him I'll be back, eh? Tell him I'll be back tomorrow.

AMANDA *follows* RAY *to the door and watches him walking away before turning back inside.*

Scene Three

NEIL *lies on the sofa reading Peter Pan. There are photographs, letters etc belonging to* RAY'*s grandmother scattered around.* RAY *sits in the middle of it, deep in thought.*

NEIL. Listen to iss . . . Mrs Darling offers to adopt Peter, and he says –

' "Would you send me to school?", he inquired craftily.

"Yes."

"And then to an office?"

"Suppose so."

"Soon I should be a man?"

"Very soon."

"I don't want to go to school and learn solemn things", he told her passionately. "I don't want to be a man. O Wendy' s mother, if I was to wake up and feel there was a beard!"

"Peter," said Wendy the comforter, "I should love you in a beard," and Mrs Darling stretched out her arms to him, but he repulsed her.

"Keep back lady, no one is going to catch me and make me a man!" '

No one is going to catch *me* and make *me* a man! I love this egotistical little bastard.

RAY. Remind you on somebody?

NEIL. Jesus Ray, take a valium for fuck sake. Ye've been lek a bear wi' a sore head since we got here.

RAY. Yeah . . . I'm sorry . . . It's all iss stuff . . . it's doing my head in. I mean shit . . . Does nobody clear up efter e dead anymore.

NEIL. I thought that was your job. You're the son and heir.

RAY. Yeah. I just never expected it all to still be here.

NEIL. Why don't ye just dump it?

RAY. What?

NEIL. Dump it. Put it in a bin liner and sling it out the back. It's noh doin you any good.

RAY. Canna chaist dump it.

NEIL. Why noh? Do ye want me to do it?

RAY. Noh, leave it be.

NEIL. It's just old shit, Ray. It's noh worth anything.

RAY. I know. Leave it though. A dinna want til throw it out.

NEIL. This is some book. "No one is going to catch me and make me a man." I remember feelin exactly lek at. Lek a wiz standing on the edge o some huge cliff and everybody I'd ever known was standing behind me shouting 'Jump! Jump! We did it. Jump!' And a'm lek – 'What? Jump off a fucking cliff? Just because you did it? Fucking crazy?' It was like somebody had actually sat down and planned out

your whole fucking life for you. Take the first job they offer
you, marry the first girl let's you fuck her, on and on, your
whole fucking life. Fucking suicide, eh?

RAY. Yeah. But we were too smart for at, eh?

NEIL. Too right we were.

RAY. Yeah, we were so fucking smart.

NEIL *watches* RAY.

NEIL. Ever thought aboot selling iss place Ray?

RAY. Selling it?

NEIL. Yeah. Taking e money and running like hell.

RAY. Who'd buy it?

NEIL. Some cunt. Some cunt wi' more money than sense. It's
what they're all looking for, is it noh? A cheap piece o
paradise.

RAY. Paradise?

NEIL. Yeah. Paradise. It's the yuppy dream. Getting away fae
it all. 'Our little place in Scotland'. They'll buy anything
nowadays.

RAY. It's noh for sale.

NEIL. Everything's for sale.

RAY. Noh. Noh everything.

NEIL (*pause*). Even if you only got ten grand for it. Ten
grand's ten grand.

RAY. Christ, do ye noh listen to me. It's noh for sale.

NEIL. Why noh?

RAY. It's ma inheritance, for fuck sake. It's supposed to mean
something. She left it to me for a reason.

NEIL. What reason?

RAY. Because she knew I'd want to live here. Someday.

NEIL. You'll never live here Ray.

RAY. Why noh?

NEIL. Ye know as well as me why noh.

Time passes. NEIL *gets up and pours himself a cup of cold tea. He watches* RAY.

NEIL. Fuck it. We'd probably be dead in a week if we ever got your hands on some real money. O.d'd in some fucked up Bangkok version o Butlins. Fuck it. Might as well stay here. Let Asia come to us. Ye takin another hit e night?

RAY. Yeah, are ye noh?

NEIL. I've got some Temazies in my bag. I think I'll try and get some sleep.

RAY. Sleep?

NEIL. Yeah, remember sleep? It's what normal people do iss time o night. Ye should try it sometime. (RAY *does not respond. Pause.*) Where did you go when ye were out? I thought ye were just going to the shop.

RAY (*shrugs*). I went up til Chaimig's. E guy in e photo.

NEIL. Yeah? How's he doin?

RAY. He's blind.

NEIL. Blind?

RAY. Yeah, blind. Chaist a blind owld man.

NEIL. Christ. How did at happen?

RAY. Fuck knows. Looked lek diabetes. His fingers were all . . . (RAY *massages his own fingers, then lets the thought go.*) He was always so strong, you know. Always. A donno. A donno what I expected.

NEIL. People get old Ray. People die. It's the way o things. It's just physics, you know. Physics or Chemistry or some shit.

RAY. Yeah, I know. I shoulda been ere for him though. Same way I shoulda been ere for ma faither . . . for ma granny . . . I donno. I donno what's happened to me lately. When did I get so fuckin selfish?

NEIL. Dinna kid yursel, Ray. Ye were always selfish.

RAY. Cheers.

NEIL. We all are. Narcissists fae way back. It's what we do. What we are. No point in crying about it now.

RAY. D'ye never get sick o it?

NEIL *seems to be considering saying something, but swallows it.*

NEIL (*pause*). I get sick o a lot o things.

RAY. Did you ever read Nietzsche Neil?

NEIL. What?

RAY. Nietzsche? E recurrance stuff? 'What if a demon should come unto you . . . '

NEIL. Yeah, I read it. Sounded lek a fairy tale to me.

RAY. Yeah, I know. I used to think I'd like it though. (*Pause.*) I said it to Christie once, you know . . . gave him the whole spiel. And what if a demon should come unto you, into your loneliest loneliness, and say – 'This life as you now live it you will have to live innumerable times more, all in the same sequence, with nothing changed; every joy, every frustration, everything, no matter how inconsequential, over and over, again and again.' Would you fall upon the ground and curse that demon, or was there a moment, a single moment, when you would have said – 'You are a god, and never have I heard anything more divine?' And Christie just looks at me – you know at look? – an he says 'I donno know who this demon thinks I am, but he's obviously got me mixed up wi' somebody who actually gives a fuck.'

RAY *laughs bitterly to himself and shakes his head.*

NEIL. You should get some sleep Ray, you're starting to worry me.

RAY. Yeah. Ye make it sound as if there was a time when I didna.

NEIL. Get some sleep, eh? I'll see you in e morning.

RAY. Yeah. If a'm noh here dinna worry. A'll chaist be doon at e shore or something.

NEIL. Yeah, okay. Take it easy, eh? Get some fucking sleep.

NEIL *exits, taking 'Peter Pan' with him. He casts a watchful eye back over* RAY. RAY *is busy getting a hit ready.* NEIL *closes the door.*

Scene Four

Next morning. Low rocks overlooking a pebble beach.
AMANDA *lies reading in the sun. In time she goes in her bag for a drink or a cigarette. As she does she finds the letter she had the previous evening, still unopened. She looks at the letter, torn between opening it and once again discarding it. She puts it back in the bag.* RAY *appears on the rocks. He doesn't see* AMANDA, *but she sees him.*

AMANDA. Don't do it Ray. Ye've got too much til live for!

RAY. Amanda? What're ye doin here?

AMANDA. Savin yur life by e look o id.

RAY. Yeah? I think I'd find a higher cliff if a wiz gonna jump.

AMANDA. Ye comin doon?

RAY. If ye dinna think it's too dangerous.

AMANDA. Chaist follow e path an dinna stray too close til e edge.

RAY. He's let ye off e leash then.

AMANDA. Yeah. He's lovely an everything, boot if a didna get awiy fie him for a couple o oors every day a'd end up stranglin him. Ye cannie strangle your grandad, can ye?

RAY. He's got a pretty thick neck.

AMANDA. Pretty thick head. He' s got an oppeenyin on everything.

RAY. He's hed a long time til collect them. (*Pause.*) It's nice here, is it noh?

AMANDA. Yeah I come here a lot. It's the only place I can get any peace.

RAY (*staring out at the waves*). We used to come here all e time. Me an Marion.

AMANDA. Yeah, I remember.

RAY. Ye remember?

AMANDA. A probably shouldna say iss. A used til follow ye sometimes.

RAY. Yeah. At's right. Ye did, did ye noh?

AMANDA. What? Ye knew?

RAY. Pit it iss way Amanda, ye wid've made a shit Indian.

AMANDA. A canna believe ye knew! Why did ye never say anything?

RAY. Love makes ye shameless. Anyway, what were ye gonna see? We were just kids.

AMANDA. I saw enough.

RAY. I doubt it.

AMANDA. I always thought ye were a good couple, ye an Marion.

RAY. Yeah, I thought so too.

AMANDA. Ye always looked . . . I donno . . .

RAY. Yeah. I know how we looked. (*Pause.*) Do ye see her much?

AMANDA. Now an again. Noh really.

RAY. She's still in Glasgow?

AMANDA. Id's a long way, ye know?

RAY. How's she doin? Is she okay?

AMANDA. She's fine. Ye know Marion. She's always fine.

RAY. A've been meaning to get in touch again. I was half hoping she'd be ere last night.

AMANDA. Noh, she disna come up much. (*Pause.*) Ye know she's merried now, do ye noh Ray?

RAY. Is she? Noh. Noh, a didna know.

AMANDA. They've got a bairn. A laskie.

RAY. Yeah? At's good. Is she happy?

AMANDA. Seems til be?

RAY. Yeah, well . . . at's always e first step towards happiness, is it noh? Gettin the fuck away fie me.

AMANDA. It wiz a long time ago Ray.

RAY. Yeah, I know . . . I'm a bit slow. Ye look a bit lek her now, ye know?

AMANDA. Do ye think?

RAY. Yeah. Different hair maybe.

AMANDA (*shrugs*). Sisters.

RAY. Yeah . . . So what ye up til? Still at school.

AMANDA. Noh, chaist feenished.

RAY. Yeah?

AMANDA. Yeah. All grown up. Five A's in ma highers. Noh it a'm boastin or anything.

RAY. Noh, course noh. Yull be leavin soon then, eh?

AMANDA. Noh, I donno. A dinna think so.

RAY. I thought that was e way it went up here. Finish school, get the fuck out.

AMANDA. It's noh at easy . . . Thurs ither things . . . A can always go in a few years. Ye can do at, can ye noh? Defer. Take a few years oot?

RAY. Yur askin e wrong person.

AMANDA. Ye never went?

RAY. Noh. A wiz shit at school. It wiz only e university o life it wid take me, but they didna hev e course I wanted.

AMANDA. Ye should've tried e school o hard knocks.

RAY. A did. It was full.

AMANDA. Maybe I will go. A donno. It's what a always wanted. What a thought a wanted. A mind when Marion went, a wiz so jealous. Couldna wait til go too.

RAY. So what's changed?

AMANDA. Thurs more til life, is thur noh? I got iss, look. (*Takes out letter.*) A've been kerryin id aroond for two days now.

RAY. Glasgow? What's at? A place?

AMANDA. Probably.

RAY. Are ye noh gonna open it?

AMANDA. A donno. A dinna want til think aboot it, tell ye e truth. Are ye gonna go up an see grandad iss efternoon?

RAY. Yeah. I said I would. Take him for at walk.

AMANDA. He's happy yur back. He willna say anything, boot ye can tell.

RAY. Yeah. A used til follow him aboot everywhere when a wiz a bairn. A mind he used til pick me up an swing me over his shoulders an ma granny wid come runnin oot shoutin – 'Fit ye doin til at bairn ya damn feel, yull make him seek', an Chaimig wid chaist laugh, gie me anither swing. A never knew what ma granny wiz worried aboot. A kent he'd never let me fall.

AMANDA. Widna let him try id now.

RAY. Noh, a dinna suppose a would.

AMANDA. Ye look tired Ray.

RAY. Yeah. A wiz up half e night goin through her things. Everything's still ere. Everything except her.

AMANDA. A miss Sadie. She wiz a lovely wifie. She wiz anither ine it used til talk aboot ye all e time.

RAY. Yeah?

AMANDA. Yeah. Ye'd think ye were e Golden Child or something. All ma life a've hed til listen til fowk goin on aboot fit a lovely loon at Raymond wiz, an all a can think is – at's e bastard used til tease me all e time coz a didna hev any tits.

RAY. Did a?

AMANDA. Too right ye did. It's a wonder a didna get a complex.

RAY. Yeah well . . . a hope a didna scar ye too badly.

AMANDA. I'll get over id.

RAY. Good. Hate til think a'd fucked up anither life. Ma granny . . . wiz thur anybody wi' her, ye know . . .

AMANDA. They took her intil e hospital. In Weeck.

RAY. Wiz it? Do ye think it wiz . . .

AMANDA. Dinna talk aboot it, eh?

RAY. Yeah, I know . . . I just wonder sometimes . . .

AMANDA. A dinna even lek thinkin aboot it.

RAY. Noh. Sorry.

AMANDA. Do ye believe in God, Ray?

RAY. God? Christ . . . What sort o question's at?

AMANDA. A straight one. Do ye?

RAY. I donno. Some days.

AMANDA. A wish a did. He's at owld now, ye know? (*Pause.*)
It scares me sometimes.

RAY (*he puts out a hand to her, supportive, unobtrusive – a
thought comes to him*). I remember iss one day doon here.
Me an Marion. We were sittin here in fact. Chaist sittin,
ye know, cuddlin up. I looked up at e sky, an a saw iss
face lookin doon, iss giant face. It wiz chaist e clouds, ye
know . . . Marion saw it too, at least she said she did. This
huge face looking doon on us. An then e wind changed and
it wiz still ere, chaist turned now, in profile. Whichever
way e clouds blew ye could still see it, iss face lookin doon
on us. Then anither one came, then anither . . . there were
aboot five o them in all, all lookin doon on us. It wiz weird,
lek a veil hed lifted. Lek we were rats in some laboratory
experiment an we'd chaist glanced up and caught sight o e
scientists looking doon at us in our cage. It felt so real, it
really did . . . and when kissed, e feeling, e feeling wiz
chaist incredible. I've never felt anything like it in ma life.
An then a heard iss voice, iss voice in ma head, sayin . . .
(*Breaking off.*) Ye think a'm mad, don't ye?

AMANDA. Noh, a dinna think yur mad.

RAY. Noh? I do.

AMANDA. What did it say?

RAY. What?

AMANDA. E voice? What did it say?

RAY. Oh . . . 'All's well', at's what it said. 'All's well. I am the guard'.

Pause

AMANDA. It's a shame.

RAY. What is?

AMANDA (*shrugs and smiles*). I donno . . .

They smile, share a moment of peace, happiness.

RAY. A suppose a'd better go an find at owld cunt, eh?

AMANDA. Yeah, wait a meenid. A'll walk ye back.

Scene Five

That afternoon. CHAIMIG *sits in* RAY's *granny's house.*

CHAIMIG. Raymond! Raymond! Are ye ere boy?

RAY (*coming through from kitchen*). Yeah. I'm here.

CHAIMIG. Div ye hev a dry paira socks?

RAY. Socks?

CHAIMIG. Aye, socks. Look at ma feet. They're sodden.

RAY. I told ye noh til go so close til e water.

CHAIMIG. Christ min, a've never listened til anither man in e whole o ma damn life. Div ye think a'm goin til start now.

RAY. Aye, had on. I've got some socks somewhere.

RAY *goes to his rucksack and takes out a pair of socks and a towel. He goes to* CHAIMIG, *takes off his socks and dries his feet.* CHAIMIG *caresses his hair.*

CHAIMIG. Yur a good loon Raymond, a good loon.

RAY. I chaist hope nobody sees me. They'll think I'm getting a Christ complex.

CHAIMIG. Ye dinna hev til annoint them wi' iyl. A chaist wanted a dry pair o socks. Aye, id's a long time since a felt e sea on ma feet. Id wis good o ye til take me. They think cause a'm blin it means niything til me, boot id's something, ken, chaist til feel e salt in e air, chaist til hear it. A spent a lot o time oot ere, wan way or anither. Div ye mind at little boatie a hed, goin oot til pick up e creels. An e herring?

RAY. Aye, a mind.

CHAIMIG. Sadie never thanked me. She always thocht ye were too sensitive a loon til be botherin wi' e sea. A telt her though. A telt her. Gie a man a fish an he'll iyt for a day, tiytch him how til fish, at's anither thing, anither thing entirely. Div ye mind Raymond? Div ye mind goin oot for e creels?

RAY. Aye, a mind. A think ma granny wiz right though. It wizna e life for me.

CHAIMIG. An fit is?

RAY. I wish I knew. I used til love it though. Bein here. I remember one time, playin up in e woods – I came til e edge o e trees. I looked down on e land, e green o e fallow, beyond at e hoose, beyond at e field ye were ploughin . . . all e way doon til e edge o e cliff . . . an above ye there wiz at huge blue sky, an e sea below ye, stretchin all e way oot til Norway, an e sun in e sky, burnin lek a pot o molten gold, white gold, burnin . . . times lek at . . . ye wish ye could live forever.

CHAIMIG. Aye min, at's e poet in ye. A wis always tellin Marion fit a great poet ye wid be. Div ye still write Raymond?

RAY. Now and again. Noh often. Things get in e way, you know?

CHAIMIG. Oh, I know. I know. But if ye've got a gift dinna squander it. Thurs plenty wid trade thur richt erms for fit ye've got. It disna come til many.

RAY. So why did it come til us?

CHAIMIG. We were blessed. Or mibbe cursed. Anyway, it left me. As mysteriously as it came it went. Mibbe thirty years an noh a word. Mibbe it knew a wizna worthy o it. It a wizna strong enough.

RAY. Christ, ye were e strongest man I ever knew.

CHAIMIG. Id's a different kind o strength Raymond . . . a different kind. E strength it can lift a bag o tatties dizna serve ye very weel when it comes til lookin intil e souls o men. Yur strong Raymond, always remember how strong ye are. If ye forget, it'll liyv ye too.

RAY. Here's yur tea. Do ye want it?

CHAIMIG. Aye, gies id here, gies id here.

CHAIMIG *puts out his hands.* RAY *places the tea in one hand, pressing* CHAIMIG'*s other hand against the cup.*

CHAIMIG. Aye, at's good. At's good. Wid ye do something for me Raymond? Wid ye read for me?

RAY. Thurs noh books here. Chaist a kid's thing.

CHAIMIG. Something o yur ain, a meant. Read something o yur ain.

RAY. I've got nothing wi' me.

CHAIMIG. Div ye noh mind thum?

RAY. Noh really. Bits an pieces.

CHAIMIG. Thur must be wan. A canna believe a poet widna ken at least wan o his poems by hert.

RAY. I'm noh really a poet.

CHAIMIG. Christ loon, div ye think a dinna ken. Yull be tellin me next a'm noh a judge.

RAY. There's one. I wrote it a long time ago.

CHAIMIG. Let's hear it then.

RAY. I donno . . . it's just a lyric, ye know . . .

CHAIMIG. Go on, min. Christ, yur worse than a wumman wi' yur ditherin.

RAY. Okay. I'll try. Ye ready.

CHAIMIG. Aye ready. Noh, fit's it called?

RAY. What?

CHAIMIG. Fit's it called. E title?

RAY. Oh. It's chaist called 'Marion'.

    And sometimes I could hear you dreaming
    As we lay in that room
    Full of unread books
    And unanswered letters
    Clock ticking lazily
    Ideas almost forming
    Then blending with the rain
    Softly falling
    Over the remnants
    Of today.

    Your face turned toward me
    Upward looking
    I stroked your hair from above.
    I loved your face
    For the thought put into it
    Every arch
    Every smile
    You never lost control
    But I could feel
    It would be good
    If you did.

    And sometimes I could hear myself dreaming
    And I'm sure you could hear it too
    As we lay in that room

Full of obituaries to dead men
We both had gently slept with
When our ideas
Seemed clear
And solid.

Vague memories of that time
Flood me with desire
Then float away
Lazy dreaming
Without retention
With you
I forget
To think.

There is a silence before CHAIMIG *speaks.*

CHAIMIG. Aye. Aye. Ye captured it. Ye captured it see. Ye pit
oot yur han an took time by e mane. Ye whispered in his ear
an calmed him. At moment, it's yurs now. Forever. Ye made
time stan still. Is at noh a wonderful thing?

RAY. Aye, but it's noh real though, is it? It's chaist words.

CHAIMIG. An are words noh enough?

RAY. Noh . . . a dinna think they are.

CHAIMIG. Yur a queer loon Raymond. They gave ye e moon
an ye wanted e stars.

RAY. Yeah, helluva thing.

CHAIMIG. An when ye get e stars, fit will ye want then?

RAY. I'll think o something.

CHAIMIG. By God, a bet ye will. A bet ye will. Thur wiz
always at restless streak in ye. At's yur granny's side. At's
Sadie through an through.

RAY. Ma granny?

CHAIMIG. Oh aye. When she wiz yowng. Aye, she wanted e
world. She thocht she'd get id too.

RAY. Wiz she noh in service? Doctor Robertson?

CHAIMIG. Oh aye, she wiz in service. Six days an wan
moarning a week she cooked an scrubbed. An on her wan
efternoon off she'd come back here an cown intil her
mithers breest. Thur must be better things, she thought.
Better things. E whole world's lookin for better things.
Noh satisfaction. Ye canna imagine it, can ye Raymond?
Yur granny a laskie, lek Marion . . . lek Amanda, bonnier
even . . . lookin oot fie e prison o her life, wantin til be
free . . . cursin e work it wiz giein her muscles lek a man,
e soft skin o her fingers turnin wrinkled an hard . . . cownin
every nicht for something better. Aye, ye should've seen
how happy she wiz when her granny selt at heefer til piy
for her passage. A wiz chaist a loon, boot a mind her pickin
me up an kissin me . . . dancin she wiz . . . an a mind how
happy she wiz . . . aye . . . an a mind when she came back . . .
Chiynged. Chiynged. Niything left o e laskie it she wiz . . .

RAY. What happened?

CHAIMIG. What happened? She never said. Boot she hed yur
faither wi' her when she came, so plenty guessed, richt or
wrong. Aye, e whole world's lookin for something better.
Except me. Except me.

NEIL *enters from outside.*

CHAIMIG. Fa's at?

RAY. Neil.

CHAIMIG. Neil boy, come in an sit. A'm tellin stories it hevna
been telt in sixty years.

NEIL. Aye.

CHAIMIG. Bliym yur pal, he got me started.

RAY. Oh, ye didna need much encouraging.

CHAIMIG. Mibbe noh, mibbe noh. Come in an sit Neil, a'm
lek at Magnusson on e telly. A've started so a'll feeneesh.

NEIL. I'll just get masel some tea.

CHAIMIG. Did a ever tell ye a kent Neil Gunn?

NEIL. What? Neil Gunn e novelist?

CHAIMIG. Aye. E novelist. E great Scottish novelist. Couldna write withoot a gless o whisky in his han. Ye could tell, could ye noh? A mind wan day sayin til him – Neil, Neil man, fit's goin on? Eight pages til catch a bloody salmon?

RAY. Aye, ye told me.

NEIL. Ye knew Neil Gunn?

CHAIMIG. Intimately.

RAY. Chaimig's a poet.

CHAIMIG. Wiz a poet. Past tense.

NEIL. I thought ye were a fairmer, a crofter . . .

CHAIMIG. Can a man noh work e land an howld a pen at e same time? Div ye think Robbie Burns wiz a librarian? At's e trouble wi' thum all nowadays. They all work in damn universities an bookshops an what hev ye. How can ye describe something ye hevna even seen? How can ye write aboot life when e only life ye've seen is books, books an more damn books. Ye willna make at mistake, will ye Raymond?

RAY. Noh much chance o at.

NEIL. There's plenty to write about here, anyway.

CHAIMIG. Here? Fit d'ye mean?

NEIL. Just e landscape. It's amazing is it noh? Everything's so bleak. I couldna believe it coming up – there's a real change . . . lek yur crossing a border. All e houses, empty, deserted, no roofs or doors, just weeds growing through e floorboards . . . but it's really beautiful at e same time, is it noh? It is . . . It is beautiful. It's funny . . .

CHAIMIG. Aye. An did ye see e ghosts Neil?

NEIL. Ghosts? (*Looking to* RAY.) What ghosts?

CHAIMIG. E ghosts o e men and women it once worked at land? E ghosts o e bairns it walked barefoot through e mountains wi' e smell o burning thatch still clingin til thur clothes? E ghosts o a happy land toarn apart by e greed an avarice o them it were entrusted til look efter id? Id's fill o ghosts Neil, fie Kildonnan til Clythe . . . id's a haunted land. Take him up til Bad biy some day Raymond. Show him e beaches they clustered on, e caves they were forced til make thur hom. Show him far they sterved. Ma mither's mither came at way. Ma faither's femly too. Ye think it wiz long ago, but it wizna long ago – id feels chaist lek yesterday til me. An id's still goin on, dinna think id's noh. They liyv an they never come back. They belong here, thur niymes tell ye at. All e Gunn's an Sinclair's an Swanson's an Sutherland's. They belong here. Boot fit's thur til stiy for, answer me at? They canna fish, they canna ferm, they canna even get jobs sellin wampum til e tourists. Ye want til stiy here ye get a job in Plutonium? Plutonium? Is at noh something? Is at noh brave new world we've beelt? A've seen fit they've done. A may be blin boot a've seen. They started wi' e crofters a hunner an fifty years ago an now id's e turn o e ships an e steel an e coal. Ye look at e highlands an ye think id's beautiful. Well id's noh beautiful – it's a prophecy. Yur livin in e land o e dispossessed, an e dis-possessed hev niything, noh even a voice. Christ, an if ye hed a voice, if ye hed a voice it could scriym an shout an scriym again, they widna hear ye . . . they widna hear . . . Do ye think a'm wrong? Yur quate ere Raymond, div ye think a'm wrong?

RAY. Noh, a dinna think yur wrong.

CHAIMIG. Noh, a'm noh wrong. A'm noh wrong . . .

RAY. A dinna think yur richt or wrong. A chaist dinna care.

CHAIMIG. Ye dinna care. Christ min, ye should damn weel care.

RAY. I know . . . I know I should . . . but a dinna.

NEIL. Ray, for fuck sake . . .

CHAIMIG. Noh Neil, let him hev his opeenyins, let him hev his apathy. A thocht better o ye though Raymond. A thocht ye'd been raised better.

RAY. I know.

CHAIMIG. Is at how id is now wi' e yowng? Noh care for far they come fie? Noh care for e pliyce they were boarn?

RAY. What's e point?

CHAIMIG. Fit's e piynt? Fit's e piynt? Christ Raymond, sometimes a'm gled a canna see.

RAY. I wish to Christ you could see, min. I wish to Christ you could.

RAY *gets up and exits. This is more in sadness than anger.*

NEIL (*stands in doorway*). Ray ... Ray ... for e love o fuck ...

CHAIMIG. Liyv him be Neil, liyv him be. He's noh a bad loon. A thocht he hed more fecht in him though, a thocht he hed more fecht.

Scene Six

NEIL *and* CHAIMIG *approach* CHAIMIG'*s house.* NEIL *is taking* CHAIMIG *home.* NEIL *helps the exhausted* CHAIMIG *in.* CHAIMIG *reaches for a chair.*

CHAIMIG. Christ min, a needed at. A canna mind e last time a walked so far.

NEIL. Ye should get a good sleep e night.

CHAIMIG. Aye, a'll sleep lek a log. Will ye take a dram Neil? Thur should be a half bottle some pliyce. Raymond took it up. When he came til see me yesterday he took it up.

NEIL. He wiz oot o order back ere. A dinna ken what his problem is.

CHAIMIG. He'll hev things on his mind noh doot. Id must be hard for e yowng nowadays. Hard til still hev any hope. Christ, ye should've seen him when he wiz a loon though. Up til all sorts. He hed something aboot him ken, a spark. A lek'd at in him, reminded me o masel.

AMANDA *enters.*

AMANDA. A thought a heard ye.

CHAIMIG. Aye, a always kent at beeg lugs o yurs wid come in handy some day.

AMANDA *makes a face/thumbs her nose.* NEIL *smiles.*

CHAIMIG. A've been oot walkin. Did ye ken at? Walkin. Miles a've walked e day. Miles. Raymond came up an took me.

AMANDA. Grandad . . . At's noh Ray.

CHAIMIG. Oh, ya cheeky bitch! Are ye hearin iss Neil? Are ye hearin fit a've got til pit up wi'? Div ye think a dinna ken fa at is? A'm blin, noh stupid.

AMANDA. Introduce us then.

CHAIMIG. Christ, is it introductions yur efter now. Neil, iss is ma grandochter Amanda, Amanda iss is Neil. He's up wi' Raymond.

NEIL. Hi.

AMANDA. Hi. Hev ye hed til pit up wi' him all day, Neil?

CHAIMIG. Pit up wi' me? Pit up wi' me? A'll hev ye ken a'm a fine conversationalist. A wealth o wisdom an information. Is at noh richt Neil? Noh many's seen an heard fit a've seen an heard.

AMANDA. Plenty's seen and heard it. They chaist dinna go til such lengths til broadcast it. Wiz he tellin ye his Neil Gunn story?

NEIL. Aye.

CHAIMIG. Here you, hev ye noh got hoosework or something til be doin? Liyv e men til thur whisky an bletherin.

AMANDA. Aye. Whisky an bletherin's all yur fit for.

CHAIMIG. A'm fit for ma denner, assumin ye've made some. And niyn o at rabbit food.

AMANDA. Yull take fit ye get. Do ye want til stiy, Neil? Thur should be plenty.

NEIL. Noh, a'd better get back. Find Ray.

AMANDA. Where is he anyway? A thocht he'd be here.

NEIL. In a strop.

CHAIMIG. He's a good loon Raymond. He's chaist got things on his mind wi' wan thing an anither.

AMANDA. What happened?

NEIL. Fuck knows. We were just talking and he took off.

CHAIMIG. A said something it musta touched a nerve. A didna mean anything.

NEIL. It's noh yur fault. He's been lek at all week. I donno what's wrong wi' him.

AMANDA. He's probably still upset aboot Christie. Must've been a shock.

CHAIMIG. Aye, at'll be fit it'll be.

NEIL. Yeah? What's Christie been up to now?

AMANDA. Did ye noh hear Neil?

NEIL. What?

AMANDA. A thocht they knew?

CHAIMIG. Raymond knew. We were sat here bletherin aboot it.

NEIL. Knew what?

AMANDA. He's dead Neil.

NEIL. What?

AMANDA. Christie's dead. He died last week. Did Ray noh
   tell ye?

ACT TWO

Scene Seven

Evening. Back at the house RAY *sits on the sofa, crouched forward, a book in his hands. He reads to himself in a voice that gradually becomes more and more tinged with bitterness.*

RAY. ' "What do you see now?"

"I don't think I see anything tonight," says Wendy, with a feeling that if Nana was here she would object to any further conversation.

"Yes you do," says Jane. "You see when you were a little girl."

"That was a long time ago, sweetheart," said Wendy. "Ah me, how time flies!"

"Does it fly," asks the artful child, "The way you flew when you were a little girl?"

"The way I flew! Do you know Jane, I sometimes wonder if I ever did really fly."

"Yes you did."

"The dear old days when I could fly!"

"Why can't you fly now mother?"

"Because I am grown up dearest. When people grow up they forget the way."

"Why do they forget the way?"

"Because they are no longer gay and innocent and heartless. It is only the gay and innocent and heartless who can fly."

"What is gay and innocent and heartless? I do wish I was gay and innocent and heartless."

Or perhaps Wendy admits that she does see something.

"I do believe," she says, 'That it is this nursery." '

NEIL *enters.*

NEIL. Why the fuck did ye noh tell me Christie was dead?

RAY. ' "I do believe it is," says Jane. "Go on." '

NEIL. Ray.

RAY. Who told ye?

NEIL. What the fuck does it matter who told me! Why did you noh tell me, at's e fucking question here? Cunt's been dead a fucking week!

RAY. Five days.

NEIL. A week, five days. Talk to me!

RAY. What?

NEIL. Why did ye noh tell me? Eh?

RAY. I tried.

NEIL. When? When did ye try?

RAY. I donno. I tried.

NEIL. I canna believe it. I canna believe you never told me about it. You should've fucking told me!

RAY. Why?

NEIL. Why?

RAY. Yeah, why? Did ye want til go til e fuckin funeral? Eh? Did ye want til kiss his mother's cheek and tell her what an A1, damn straight guy her son was? How kind he was? How generous? How maybe he widna gie ye a score if you were really fucking sick but at least he'd let you boil up his filters? Get real for fuck sake. He's dead, we're alive. End of story, end of argument. Another dead junkie, who fucking cares?

NEIL. He was your best mate for fucksake! You grew up together.

RAY. He died. It's only pricks who die.

NEIL. Ray! Talk to me! Just tell me what happened for fuck's sake!

RAY. Did they noh tell ye? It was in e paper. Local man drowns. It's funny. Local men have been drowning for centuries. They never get tired o at one.

NEIL. So it's true. He did droon. I thought . . .

RAY. He drooned. He was doon in e sooth of Spain and he drooned. Happens every day . . . Some cunt goes swimming after a heavy meal, after drinking too much cheap booze, after jacking up a couple of barbs.

NEIL. He was stoned?

RAY. What do ye think? They found traces o something in his blood. Could've been old. Get real. Cunt couldna cross e street without being fucked up on something.

NEIL. Jesus Ray . . .

RAY. What? What? Dinna look at me? A dinna hev e answers!

NEIL. Is this what all this is about?

RAY. What?

NEIL. Coming back here? Talking about getting clean? You're scared . . .

RAY. Scared? Scared o what? Is your life so rich that losin it scares ye? At's just your genes twitchin, your DNA screaming oot for replication. That's noh how ye really feel. We've been chasing death our entire fucking lives. That's what we do. We're in love wi' e idea o our own deaths. We're such shitty fucking egotists it even turns us on. We actually think we'll be up ere watching . . . listening to them, eavesdropping our own fucking funerals . . . Ye know – 'How tragic' 'Such a waste' And we're up there laughing at

them. Jesus! Everything recoils from death. Every animal
on this entire fucking planet. What sort of animal recoils
from life? Eh? What sort o animal's at?

NEIL. Jesus. Christie eh? I didna even know he could swim.

RAY. He couldna.

NEIL. So what was he doin' out in e water?

RAY. I remember this clear as yesterday. We'd be about
fifteen/sixteen. Sitting about in his bedroom, drinking wine,
blowing dope, playin guitar. Christie's lying on his bed, and
he says – he's fifteen years old – and he says 'Ray, did I
ever tell you I was gonna kill myself'. I just laughed. He
started laughing too. Both fucking stoned.

NEIL. What? You're saying . . . Ye think he killed himsel?

RAY. I know he killed himsel.

NEIL. Noh. I dinna believe ye, there's no way . . . Noh . . .
There's no way he would've killed himsel . . .

RAY. Ye never even knew him, did ye?

NEIL. I knew him. I knew him better then you by the sound o it.
He loved life. That's what this whole thing was aboot . . .
living it, pushing it . . . nah . . . no way did he kill himsel . . .
No way.

RAY. You want to know how much Christie loved life? You
want to know? He loved it so much he swallowed a handful
of downers and walked into the sea. He walked into the sea
and opened his big, fat mouth and he swallowed the whole
fucking ocean.

NEIL. No.

RAY. Yes.

NEIL. It was an accident.

RAY. It wasna a fucking accident. I got a postcard from him. A
postcard from a dead man. Know what it said? 'Going for a
swim. If anybody asks tell them it was something trivial.'

Tell them it was something trivial. Jesus . . . Cunt! Stupid! Fucking! Cunt!

Pause.

NEIL. Jesus Ray.

RAY. Don't fucking touch me.

NEIL. Ray . . .

RAY. I mean it. Keep away fie me.

RAY *picks up his jacket.*

NEIL. Where ye goin?

RAY. I'm goin for a fucking swim.

NEIL. Ray! Shit!

NEIL *takes his frustration out on the coffee table, which he kicks viciously.*

NEIL. Shit!

Scene Eight

Late at night. CHAIMIG *stands outside his house, looking out at the land, you would think, if it wasn't for the fact he is blind.* NEIL *picks through the debris in the house, looking for his works, kicking out at anything that reminds him of his frustration. In time he cooks up a hit.* AMANDA *comes out to empty the remains of their meal into the dustbin. Her action coincides with* NEIL *lashing out at inanimate objects in the house. She/*NEIL *disturbs* CHAIMIG's *reverie.*

CHAIMIG. Amanda?

AMANDA. Aye, fa did ye think it wiz?

CHAIMIG. A thocht it wiz ye, at's why a sayed yur niyme.

AMANDA *goes to join him, listening to the quiet of the night.*

AMANDA. A thocht ye'd gone til yur bed.

CHAIMIG. Noh. A'm chaist stannin here. Chaist thinkin.

AMANDA. Fit ye thinkin aboot?

CHAIMIG. Oh . . . many wonders, as is my wont.

AMANDA. Yur fill o magic, are ye noh?

CHAIMIG. Oh aye, a'm a reegular bag o tricks. Thurs a bird oot ere, can ye hear id? Damned if a can pit ma finger on id.

AMANDA. They all sound e same til me.

CHAIMIG. My, at's a sad state o affairs.

AMANDA. A ken fit a skorry sounds lek. At's aboot it.

CHAIMIG. Everybody kens fit a skorry sounds lek. Div ye ken fit e principle diet o e skorry is Amanda?

AMANDA. A donno. Fish?

CHAIMIG. Hamburgers! Is at noh something. A heard a mannie on e wireless say id. E principle diet o e skorry is e hamburger.

AMANDA. Is at fit ye've been stannin here thinkin aboot?

CHAIMIG. Christ noh. Yur e ine started talkin aboot skorries. Noh, a wiz thinkin aboot something else. Aye, something else entirely.

AMANDA. Time ye were thinkin aboot bed.

CHAIMIG. Aye, mibbe. A'm tired enough for it. A dinna ken Amanda. Mibbe id wizna such a good idea, walkin so far iss efternoon.

AMANDA. Ye hed a good time though?

CHAIMIG. Aye. Good enough. A'm piyin for id now though.

AMANDA. Id wiz good o Ray til take ye.

CHAIMIG. Aye. Aye, it wiz good o him.

AMANDA. Ye miss him, do ye noh?

CHAIMIG. A miss e boyig he wiz. (*Pause.*) Thurs a chiynge in him, hev ye noticed?

AMANDA. In Ray? Noh . . . Fit sort o chiynge?

CHAIMIG. A dinna ken. Chaist a chiynge.

AMANDA. He's been awiy a while. Thurs bound til be a chiynge.

CHAIMIG. Aye, mibbe at's fit it is. Mibbe e chiynge is in me. A donno. Id's funny Amanda, ye think yull always be yursel, noh maitter fit. Ye think yull always be yursel, then wan day ye realise yur noh.

AMANDA. So what else are ye?

CHAIMIG. A donno. Something else. Something ye never thocht ye'd be.

AMANDA. Yur still e same as ye always were. Yur chaist tired.

CHAIMIG. Aye, a'm tired.

AMANDA. Come on in. A'll get ye some tea.

CHAIMIG. Noh, a'll stiy oot here a bit yet. Id'll come til me. A'll mind fit id is.

AMANDA. Dinna be too long.

AMANDA goes to go back inside. CHAIMIG's voice stops her in her tracks.

CHAIMIG. A dinna want ye wiystin yur life on me, Amanda. Ye ken at, div ye noh? (*Pause.*) A dinna want me howldin ye back.

AMANDA. Yur noh howldin me back. Fit put at intil yur hiyd?

CHAIMIG. A dinna ken. Yur lek e birds, are ye noh? Ye all fly sooth.

She goes back to him and cuddles him.

AMANDA. Yur an owld fool sometimes, ye ken at?

CHAIMIG. Id widna surprise me. A wizna at bricht when a wiz yowng. A mean id though. A dinna want ye wiystin yur life on me.

AMANDA. Come on. Yur chaist tired. Ye've hed a long day.

CHAIMIG. Aye. Thur never long enough though, are they? Never long enough.

> CHAIMIG *turns and walks away.* AMANDA *watches him then follows.* NEIL'*s voice is heard from the kitchen of* RAY'*s granny's house.*

NEIL. Nnnnunph . . .

> *Blood drips down his outstretched arm. His eyes close. He drops the syringe in his hand.*

Scene Nine

NEIL *is slumped in the kitchen, apparently od'd. A knock comes to the door. He does not react. The knock comes again.* NEIL *stirs slightly. The knock comes again, followed by* AMANDA'*s voice. She will enter of her own accord.*

AMANDA (*off*). Ray? Ye in ere?

> NEIL *gets to his feet. He's not in a good way.*

NEIL. Wha . . .? Shit . . .

AMANDA. Ray?

NEIL. He's noh here!

AMANDA. Neil . . . is Ray here?

NEIL. Noh. Noh, he's noh here.

AMANDA. Where is he?

NEIL. Do ye noh listen?

AMANDA. Yeah, I heard. Jesus Neil . . . Are ye okay?

NEIL. Yeah. I'm fine.

AMANDA. Jesus Neil . . .

NEIL. What?

AMANDA. Iss pliyce . . .

NEIL. What can I say? We live like pigs.

AMANDA. What happened? Where's Ray?

NEIL. Fuck Ray.

AMANDA. Neil . . .

NEIL. What?

AMANDA. What's goin on? Tell me.

NEIL. Tell you what? I donno what's going on! I've been tryin
to work it oot masel! Christ! I mean . . . Ye come up here for
a coupla days . . . a coupla days peace and quiet . . . a coupla
days away fae all at shite . . . an what do ye get, eh? What do
ye get? More fucking shite! Ten times the amount o shite!
Jesus! I mean e cunt's been dead a fucking week. Cunt's
been dead a fucking week and he disna even fuckin tell me.

NEIL *lashes out at some convenient objects, ornaments, the
coffee table etc*

AMANDA. Christie?

NEIL. Yeah, Christie! Christ! Do ye remember when friend-
ship meant something? Do ye? I do. Friends? Jesus. Cunts it
didna die on me wouldna even fuckin shit on me . . .

AMANDA. Ye okay?

NEIL *is holding his hand.*

NEIL. Yeah. Fine.

AMANDA. Jesus, fit a miyss.

NEIL. Yeah, what a fucking mess. What ye doin here anyway?
Did yur mother never tell ye to stay away from strange
men?

AMANDA. A wiz lookin for Ray.

NEIL. Who did ye think a wiz talkin aboot? Ray? Jesus . . .
What do ye want him for?

AMANDA. A chaist wanted til speak til him. It's noh
important. Do ye know where he is?

NEIL. He's oot ere somewhere. Go an look for him if ye want.

AMANDA. Where oot ere? Did he noh say anything?

NEIL. He said he was going for a swim. Aw, I donno.
Wherever he is I hope he fucking croaks.

AMANDA. Ye dinna mean at.

NEIL. I mean it all right.

NEIL *goes to pick up his bag which is behind* AMANDA.
AMANDA *backs off.*

NEIL. What? Ye thought I was gonna hurt ye?

AMANDA. Noh.

NEIL. Ye did. Ye thought I was gonna hurt ye. Jesus. Who do
ye think I am? Jesus. I'm noh goin t' hurt ye. Only person
gettin hurt round here is me.

AMANDA. What happened Neil?

NEIL. Nothing happened.

NEIL *grabs his bag and starts stuffing his things into it.*

AMANDA. What ye doin?

NEIL. What does it look lek?

AMANDA. Yur leaving?

NEIL. Yeah, I'm leavin. I mean, it's been really peachy being a
guest in your lovely fucking country and everything but
right now I've got to get back to somewhere a little less
fucked up.

AMANDA. At iss time?

NEIL (*continues packing*). Yeah well, you know what they say.

AMANDA. Thurs noh buses or trains, Neil, noh traffic on e
road. Yull get nowhere.

NEIL. I am nowhere.

AMANDA. What about Ray?

NEIL. Fuck Ray.

AMANDA. Whatever happened . . .

NEIL. What the fuck do you know about what happened?

AMANDA. Just wait Neil. Wait til e moarning. Thur'll be a
bus at six. It'll take ye wherever ye want til go.

NEIL. Christ Amanda, buses dinna go where I want to go.

NEIL *breaks down a little.*

AMANDA. Sit doon Neil, eh . . . Chaist sit . . . I'll make some
tea.

NEIL. All the tea in China, eh? All the tea in china cups.

NEIL *throws his bag away and sits, exhausted, close to
tears.* AMANDA *goes tentatively to make tea, still unsure
of what is going on. She notices something in the doorway
and kneels down to pick it up.*

AMANDA. Neil . . .

NEIL *looks up.* AMANDA *has his discarded syringe in her
hand.*

AMANDA. Is iss yurs?

NEIL (*under breath*). Shit.

Scene Ten

CHAIMIG*'s house.* CHAIMIG *is slouched over the table, his head resting in his arms. There is an empty glass on the table beside him.* RAY *pushes open the already opened door, tapping lightly as he does. He sees* CHAIMIG.

RAY (*softly*). Chaimig . . .

He approaches CHAIMIG *tentatively, unsure for a moment if he is sleeping or dead.*

RAY. Chaimig?

CHAIMIG *comes awake.*

CHAIMIG. Fit? Fa's at? Fa's ere?

RAY. It's me. Ray. Raymond. It's okay.

CHAIMIG. Raymond?

RAY. Aye, it's chaist me.

CHAIMIG. Raymond? Christ . . . a wiz driymin ere . . . a thocht . . . Raymond? Fit ye doin here? Far's Amanda?

RAY. A donno. A chaist saw yur lights.

CHAIMIG. Lichts?

RAY. Aye, yur lit up lek a beacon.

CHAIMIG. Christ . . . A wiz driymin ere . . . a thocht a saw him . . . a thocht . . . Is Amanda noh wi' ye?

RAY. Noh, it's chaist me.

CHAIMIG. She's noh here.

RAY. Noh, she must've gone oot somewhere.

CHAIMIG. Oot? Aye . . . She's chaist gone oot . . . Far am a? Wiz a sleepin?

RAY. Aye, sparked oot at e table.

CHAIMIG. Christ, a canna take ma whisky e way a used til. A'm an owld man, boot time a fuckin realised id. Is ma fags ere?

RAY. Aye, here. Ye got it.

RAY *gives* CHAIMIG *a Woodbine and lights it once it is in* CHAIMIG*'s mouth.*

CHAIMIG. Aye, at's better. Far are we now?

RAY. A chaist thought a'd come in an see ye. A'm sorry aboot iss efternoon Chaimig.

CHAIMIG. Iss efternoon? Fit happened iss efternoon.

RAY. A donno. A'm sorry anyway. A dinna ken fit's wrong wi' me anymore.

CHAIMIG. Christ loon, ye dinna need til appologise til me.

RAY. Noh?

CHAIMIG. A've kent ye yur whole life Raymond. Thurs niything bad in ye. Niything bad. Div ye ever read e bible Raymond?

RAY. E bible?

CHAIMIG. Aye, ye ken fit e bible is, div ye noh? Ma faither used til read id til us, every nicht, withoot fail. 'Let not yur heart be troubled', at wiz ma favourite ine. 'Let not your heart be troubled; ye believe in God believe also in me. In my father's house there are many mansions; if it were not so I would have told you. I go to prepare a place for you. And if I go to prepare a place for you then I will come again and receive you unto myself, that where I am there ye may be also'. Is at noh beautiful Raymond? A always thocht at wiz beautiful.

RAY. Aye, it is. It is beautiful.

CHAIMIG. Course a dinna believe a damned word o id.

RAY. Noh?

CHAIMIG. Not wan damn word. Id's a lullaby see. A lullaby. Something ye sing til e bairns til get thum off til sleep.

RAY. A wiz mindin ere when a wiz a bairn. At time a got lost up in Mertin's field. D'ye mind? A wiz stannin ere cryin ma eyes oot, an then ye appeared stridin oot lek ye owned e land. A ran til ye, an ye went – 'Mercy loon, fit ye cownin for now?' – an a said – 'A'm loast. A'm cownin cause a'm loast' and ye chaist took ma han an said – 'Come on now. Ye micht be loast, boot a ken e way' De ye mind? Chaimig, I'm loast again.

CHAIMIG. Fa wiz at now?

RAY. At wiz ye, ye an me?

CHAIMIG. Wiz it now? Christ, at must've been a while ago.

RAY. Aye it wiz, it wiz a while ago. Chaimig a'm goin back tomorrow. It's been good seein ye again.

CHAIMIG. Here now, dinna go. Dinna go withoot a dram. A'll noh hev fowk sayin they came til visit Chaimig Swanson an went hom withoot a dram.

RAY. Okay. Just the one.

CHAIMIG. Aye, at's e way. Wull hev a dram. Thurs a half bottle here some pliyce. Can ye see id?

RAY. Aye, a'll get it.

CHAIMIG. Id's aroond here some pliyce. Raymond took id up. When he came up e ither nicht he took id up.

RAY. Chaimig?

CHAIMIG. Fit?

RAY (*shaking head*). Disna maitter.

CHAIMIG. Hev ye found id?

RAY. Aye, it's here. Thurs noh much left.

CHAIMIG. Thur'll be enough for a dram surely?

RAY. Aye, enough for a dram.

Scene Eleven

Back at the house. AMANDA *sits, looking across at* NEIL.
She holds the copy of Peter Pan lightly in her hand. NEIL *is
huddled in a blanket, staring down at the floor, very subdued.*

AMANDA. Ye feelin better now Neil?

NEIL. Yeah, I'm fine . . . thanks.

AMANDA. We' better tidy iss pliyce before Ray gets back.

NEIL. Noh, leave it. (*Pause.*) It's chaist owld shit. It's noh
worth anything.

AMANDA. It's Sadie's.

NEIL. Yeah well . . . if she was here I'd tidy it up.

AMANDA *gets up, starts putting things back in their
places.*

NEIL. Leave it Amanda, eh? I'll do it.

NEIL *gets to his feet, starts tidying up.*

NEIL. Ye know e funny thing. I only came up here because
I was worried about him. I was worried about *him*. Jesus.
It was even me who said it. Let's get oot o here. Piss off.
Get some peace and quiet or something. I thought we were
family, you know . . . me, him, Christie. Just shows ye, eh?
Just shows ye . . .

AMANDA. A mind at guy Christie. A used til see him wi'
Marion and Ray sometimes. There wiz something aboot
him . . . A donno . . . there wiz chaist something aboot him
it didna seem right. He didna seem til fit.

NEIL. None o us fit. That's why we were friends. Freaks.
Fucking freaks running around spoiling everybody's fun.
Yeah, at's us . . . Freaks. I used to think that was great, you
know? Being a freak. You're outside anyway, ye might as
well make out like it's what you wanted to be. Like it was a
choice.

AMANDA. Why do ye do it Neil? Why'd ye take at stuff?

NEIL. Christ Amanda, if ye've got to ask.

AMANDA. A want til know.

NEIL. I take it because it's real. I thought it was real. I thought it was serious. I thought it was the only serious thing left.

AMANDA. Thurs lots o serious things. Thurs more to life than sticking a needle in yur airm.

NEIL. At least then ye feel it. At least then ye know yur fucking alive.

AMANDA. Ye dinna hev til kill yursel til know yur alive.

NEIL. Maybe ye do. Maybe nowadays ye do. Christ, I remember one night I was sitting in wi' Christie . . . he was reading this book . . . it was a biography o Ned Kelly. All o a sudden he just threw it across the room, and I looked at him, and he was crying. There were tears in his eyes, and he said – 'There's no frontiers. There's nothing left'. And he was crying. What are ye supposed to do, eh? What are ye supposed to do when there's nothing left to do.

Pause.

AMANDA. Did ye never think o goin til university Neil?

NEIL. What?

AMANDA. University. Studying. Ye could've . . . yur noh stupid.

NEIL. Never really came up. Ye know, dad, can ye take yur cock oot o ma mooth for a minute, I want to discuss my future.

AMANDA. What?

NEIL. Forget it. I'm joking.

AMANDA. Jokes are supposed to be funny, Neil.

NEIL. Yeah, I know. I'm out of practice. Is that what you're gonna do then? Fuck off to college.

AMANDA. Noh. A'm stayin here.

NEIL. What happened? Did they have a 'No Teuchters' policy at Oxford?

AMANDA. A widna know. It was Glasgow a wiz gonna go til.

NEIL. Fuck up your exams?

AMANDA. Noh. A got them. A wiz gonna go. A even applied. (*Takes out letter.*) A got iss e ither day.

NEIL. What is it?

AMANDA. It's fie e university.

NEIL. Are ye noh gonna open it?

AMANDA. Noh. Disna maitter now. A'm noh goin. Ye know why a'm at ma grandad's, Neil? Ma mither wiz gonna put him in a hom. He canna look efter himsel, an social services willna put somebody oot every day. A hed til tell him a needed peace an quate til study. He's got no idea.

NEIL. Ye canna gie up yur life for his.

AMANDA. Why noh?

NEIL. I donno.

AMANDA. It would break his heart, ye know? Of course, if a dinna go it might break mine.

NEIL. Ye must really love him.

AMANDA (*shrugs*). Call it what ye want.

RAY *has appeared in the doorway.*

RAY. Who do you love?

AMANDA. I love you Ray. Always have done.

NEIL. Where the fuck have you been?

RAY. Thought I'd gie ye time til cool off. Ye goin somewhere?

NEIL. Home.

RAY. Didna know ye hed one.

RAY has just come in and instinctively started to cook up.

AMANDA. Ah Christ, dinna do at in front o me.

RAY. Go then.

NEIL. Dinna talk to her lek at.

RAY. Noh, sorry . . . (*Shrugs.*) Neccessity makes beasts of us all.

AMANDA. What happened til ye Ray.

RAY. Fuck knows. Whatever it wiz ye'd've thought they'd've put a lable on it. Oh, a went in til see Chaimig. He'd fallen asleep at e kitchen table. All e lights were blazin.

AMANDA. Is he all right?

RAY. Yeah. I put him to bed. How long's he been lek at?

AMANDA. Fit? Blind?

RAY. Noh, e ither thing.

AMANDA. Fit ither thing? A dinna ken fit yur talkin aboot.

RAY stops cooking up and falls back on the floor, exhausted. He talks to NEIL, excluding AMANDA.

RAY. Oh fuck . . . Christ man, clock's tickin. Time's runnin oot. A can feel it.

NEIL. Dinna talk shite.

RAY. No shit. A can feel it . . . A can feel it on e back o ma neck. Christ, a hevna slept in days.

NEIL. Christ Ray, this has got to end.

RAY. It never ends.

NEIL. It's got to. I'm gonna see about a programme when I get back. Chuck it for good. Come wae me eh?

RAY. A programme willna help ye. Ye want til do it thurs only wan way.

NEIL. I couldna handle it. Noh cold.

RAY (*going back to cooking up*). Yur noh gonna do it then, are ye? It's chaist more junkie bullshit.

NEIL. Fuck! I am so sick o you!

RAY. Yeah. Join e club. Christ, amount o nights I've sat up listening to some snivelling little cunt goin on aboot what he's gonna do when he kicks. They never do.

NEIL. I'm serious.

RAY. Everybody's serious til their bones start to ache.

AMANDA. What were ye talkin aboot Ray? Fit ither thing?

RAY. Christ Amanda. Ye know. Ye live wi' him.

AMANDA. What?

RAY. He's goin senile for fuck sake.

AMANDA. He is not.

RAY. Kicking's easy. It's what you do next that's hard.

AMANDA. Ray!

RAY. What?

AMANDA. He's noh goin senile!

RAY. Okay. He's noh goin senile. (*Pause.*) It's chaist gonna get worse, Amanda, ye know at, don't ye?

AMANDA *slaps* RAY *hard, then rushes out.*

NEIL. Prick.

NEIL *goes after* AMANDA. RAY *sits rock like, still absorbing the slap. A tear comes to his eye. He has a full syringe in his hand. Slowly, almost unconsciously, he eases down on the plunger and the heroin seeps out onto the floor. The syringe falls from his hand. In a fit of rage he sweeps his other hand across the table, spilling the remaining heroin on the floor. He breaks down.*

Scene Twelve

The next morning. RAY huddles on the sofa, shivering slightly. He has had a long, dark, torturous night. Like a drowning man he has watched his life pass before his eyes and he has considered his own death. He is not in a good way, but now and again something flickers in him, some new resolve or hope. He has turned his eyes back towards life. But it's been a long time since his last hit and he's starting to get sick. He can't find any peace. The door swings open. It's NEIL.

RAY. Neil.

NEIL. I'm just back for my bag.

RAY. Where've ye been?

NEIL. Amanda's. I crashed on her sofa.

RAY. What're you doing?

NEIL. There's a bus at twelve.

RAY. Neil . . . I'm sorry, eh?

NEIL. Yeah. We're all sorry.

RAY. Noh. seriously . . . I'm sorry . . . I'm sorry for everything . . . I really am. Jesus Neil . . . I've done something really stupid.

NEIL. Christ Ray, ye look lek shit.

RAY. Should see it fie this side. Feels worse than it looks.

NEIL. Are ye ill?

RAY. What do ye think?

NEIL. I dunno. I'm noh a doctor.

RAY. Wish ye were. Christ Neil, I did something really fucking stupid.

NEIL *sees empty wrap.*

NEIL. Ye finished it?

RAY. Noh. I dropped it. Dropped it or threw it away.
Something lek at. A hevna hed a hit since yesterday.

NEIL. Christ Ray, here. (*Offers up his drugs.*)

RAY. Noh.

NEIL. Take it.

RAY. A dinna want it.

NEIL. Course ye do.

RAY. Noh, it's over. It's over.

NEIL. What? Yur kicking?

RAY. How hard can it be?

NEIL. Jesus Ray, yur mad. If it was me . . . Christ . . . Look,
take a hit, get on e bus . . . we'll find a programme when we
get back . . .

RAY. Thurs only wan way til do it, Neil. Ye know as well as
me. Noh easy answers, eh?

NEIL. Jesus Ray . . . I donno what to say.

RAY. How about 'Good luck'?

NEIL. Yeah, good luck . . . Jesus . . .

RAY. Neil . . . I'm sorry about last night, eh?

NEIL. Yeah. Ye should've told me.

RAY. Yeah. I know.

NEIL. Why the fuck did ye noh tell me?

RAY. What good would it have done?

NEIL. What good? Christ Ray, did ye noh think a hed a right
to know? He was my friend for fuck sake.

RAY. I know. I know he was. I was just so mad . . . He used to
say to me ye know . . . he used to say – 'Look oot ere, see

what they're doing? They're building a wall.' And he was
right. One by one they were taking everybody we knew and
moulding them into bricks for their wall. But noh us, ye
know? They could never get us. Well they got him. As soon
as he walked into the water they got him. Now he's just
another brick. Another brick walling me in. Maybe that's all
he ever wiz.

NEIL. Noh.

RAY. Feels lek it.

NEIL. He was one o us.

RAY. Yeah. He was one o us. Whatever he was he was one of
us. A hed a choice til make wance. Probably e only real
choice a ever hed in ma life. A hed til choose between him
and a woman. I chose him.

NEIL. What do ye mean ye chose him?

RAY. I chose him. He went wan way, she went e ither. A hed
til choose which one I followed. I chose him.

NEIL. Marion?

RAY. A thought she'd follow me. A thought she loved me at
much. Stupid eh?

NEIL. Yeah, pretty stupid.

RAY. Ye know e stupidest thing? E stupidest thing o all? All at
stuff we used til laugh at, all e stuff we thought we were
rebelling against, that's all I want now. I want a wife. I want
kids. I want to grow up and be a man. Is at noh e stupidest
thing ye've ever heard in your entire fucking life?

RAY *is exhausted. He sits back and closes his eyes.*

RAY. I hope he's okay.

NEIL. Who?

RAY. Christie. Wherever he is I hope he's okay.

NEIL. D'ye want some tea?

RAY. All the tea in China.

NEIL. All the tea in China cups.

RAY. Are ye noh goin til miss yur bus?

NEIL. I'm noh goin. I'll see ye through, then you do the same for me.

RAY. Yeah. Okay. If at's what ye want?

NEIL. I want a yacht in Monte Carlo and a blow job off at lassie on Blue Peter. Let's chaist do it, eh? Work out what we want later.

NEIL *picks up* AMANDA'*s letter.*

RAY. What's at?

NEIL. Amanda's. She must've left it last night. She's something, eh?

RAY. Who? Amanda?

NEIL. Yeah. Giving it all up to look after her grandfaither.

RAY. What's she giving up?

NEIL. She wiz gonna go off to University. Glasgow. At's what iss is. Her letter of acceptance. Or rejection I suppose.

RAY. She's noh opened it yet?

NEIL. She's noh goin to leave him whatever it says. At's something, eh?

RAY. Christ, she should go.

NEIL. Why?

RAY. There's nothing for her here.

NEIL. More than we've got.

RAY. Yeah, more than we've got.

NEIL *goes to make the tea.*

RAY. Neil . . .

NEIL. Yeah.

RAY. Nothing, eh.

NEIL. Yeah.

> RAY *picks up* AMANDA*'s letter and looks at it. He sits with it for a while, considering something. Then he opens the letter*

Scene Thirteen

The beach. AMANDA *is there, reading.* RAY *appears. He tosses down a pebble to catch her attention then follows it down.*

RAY. Hi.

AMANDA. What do ye want?

RAY. Chaist wanted til see ye.

AMANDA. Maybe a dinna want til see ye Ray. Did ye ever think o at?

RAY. Yeah. It crossed ma mind.

AMANDA. Christ, look at ye. A canna believe what's happened til ye.

RAY. Noh, sometimes a hev trouble wi' it masel. A'm sorry aboot last night. A chaist wanted til tell ye at.

AMANDA. What part o last night?

RAY. Whichever part needs apologisin for.

> RAY *sits on a rock, shivering, looking out at the sea.*

RAY (*takes letter*). Here. Ye left at at the house. I thought ye might need it. Ye got in.

AMANDA. What the fuck you doin opening my letters. Fuck! (*Takes it, reads it, then crumples up the letter.*)

RAY. Yur really doin it then?

AMANDA. What?

RAY. Stayin here. Giein up e chance o goin til University so ye can look efter him.

AMANDA. Yeah, a'm really doin it. What am a supposed to do? Put him in a hom?

RAY. Ye've got til think o yursel.

AMANDA. E way ye do.

RAY. Christ Amanda, do ye think a'm proud o e life a've led?

AMANDA. Yeah, I do. I think ye are proud. I think ye think it makes ye special or something. It disna. Ye know at, don't ye. Chaist makes ye pathetic.

RAY. Christ . . . Wur noh talkin aboot me here. It's yur future. Do ye noh want to go or what?

AMANDA. Course a want to go. Course a do. Boot it wid kill him, goin intil a hom. Ye know it would.

RAY. Yeah, I know. (*Pause.*) Hev ye thought iss through, Amanda. Hev ye thought how it'll be a couple o years doon e line. Stuck oot in at hoose in e middle o winter wi' niything boot a blind owld man for company. Yu'll end up hating him, Amanda. Yu'll end up hating everything.

AMANDA. Chaist lek ye then.

RAY. Ye dinna want til end up lek me.

AMANDA. He's noh senile. He gets confused, at's all. He's noh senile.

RAY. Noh. I got it wrong. A wiz pissed off. Pissed off wi' everything. Ye chaist got in e way. Ye should go though, ye really should.

AMANDA. A canna go. A canna chaist leave him. A canna chaist leave him lek everybody else did.

Pause

RAY. I'll look efter him.

AMANDA. Ye?

RAY. Yeah, me. Why noh? He wiz lek a faither til me. He wiz more o a faither than ma ain faither wiz. (*Pause.*) A'm coming back, Amanda. A'm kicking junk an coming back for good. A'll look efter him.

AMANDA. Yur dreamin Ray.

RAY. Maybe a am. Maybe a think e world owes me wan last dream.

AMANDA. Ye couldna look efter him Ray.

RAY. Why noh?

AMANDA. Ye dinna love him.

RAY. Ye dinna know what I feel.

AMANDA. Ye dinna feel anything, Ray. At's yur trouble.

RAY. At's funny, a always thought ma trouble was it a felt too much. Think aboot it anyway. A'll be here, noh maitter fit.

RAY *leaves, before* AMANDA.

AMANDA *has picked up the letter, reads it, leaves.*

Scene Fourteen

Transition. Time passing. Music. RAY *paces the room, breathing heavily, the sickness kicking in. He reacts physically against the pain and mental turmoil. Whatever he does he can't get free.* CHAIMIG *sits at the kitchen table.* AMANDA *comes in.*

AMANDA. Grandad . . . Can I talk til ye.

RAY *screams like an animal.* NEIL *comes rushing in.*

NEIL. Ray . . . Jesus . . . are you alright?

RAY. Oh Christ Neil, iss is hard.

NEIL. Yeah, I know, I know.

RAY. What do ye fucking know?

NEIL. Christ Ray, I've been sick. I know what it feels like.

RAY. Noh lek iss ye've noh.

NEIL. Noh. Noh lek iss.

RAY. Christ Neil . . . gie me something eh?

NEIL. Noh.

RAY. Come on min. Chaist a needle, eh? I'll shoot up water or something. I'll shoot up salt. A chaist need a needle in me.

NEIL. Noh, leave it, eh? Here, take some jellies eh? Might calm ye down.

RAY. Noh . . . I need . . . I need . . . Oh fuck Neil.

NEIL. Yeah, I know. Come on. Put it oot yur mind eh? Put it oot yur mind.

RAY. How, for fuck's sake?

NEIL. I donno, Christ. Think happy thoughts.

RAY. Happy thoughts. Jesus, ye crack me up sometimes, ye know at?

NEIL. I'm doin ma fuckin best. Iss is hard for me too.

RAY. Yeah? Put me oot ma misery then.

NEIL. Noh. Come on man. Yur gonna do iss. I'm gonna make sure ye do iss.

RAY. Christ Neil, hev ye any idea fit iss feels lek?

NEIL. Yeah I know. Forget it, eh? Forget it. Start thinking about what it's gonna be lek when it's over.

RAY. It's never going to be over.

NEIL. Yeah it will . . . Think aboot at. E things yur gonna do.

RAY. What things?

NEIL. I donno. Stupid things, normal things.

RAY. Christ man, I donno what's normal any more.

NEIL. All at nights ye were sitting gowchin, what were ye thinking aboot? What was goin through your head?

RAY. I donno man. Smurfs. I used to think about smurfs a lot.

NEIL. Jesus, you're more fucked up than I thought.

RAY. King Freak eh? Phew . . . God . . . it's passing.

He crawls across the floor on his belly, pain etched across his face. He flips onto his back, arms stretched, gazing up at the roof.

NEIL. Okay?

RAY. Yeah, it's passing, it's passing . . .

NEIL. Ride it oot, eh? Ride it oot . . . It'll be over soon, eh?

RAY. Yeah.

Lights dip

CHAIMIG *is lit, Standing at the front of his house, as at the beginning of Scene Eight.*

His thoughts are far away and sad. AMANDA *comes out to him and stands near by. She touches his back sadly, just brushing it, taking her hand away.* CHAIMIG *puts his arm out to her and* AMANDA *cuddles into him. Meanwhile back at the house* RAY *paces and struggles. Daylight starts to emerge through the curtained window.* RAY *falls back on the sofa and pulls an old blanket around him.*

NEIL *comes in with tea.*

RAY. Oh God man, that's good. How much sugar?

NEIL. Six spoons.

RAY. Oh great. Chaist e way a lek it.

NEIL. How ye doin?

RAY. Better.

NEIL. Jellies kicking in?

RAY. Yeah. Gie me some more.

NEIL *passes the pill jar.* RAY *puts a few in his mouth and swallows. He gets unsteadily to his feet, but as soon as he does the pain comes upon him again and he doubles up.* RAY *lies back.* NEIL *gets to his feet and wanders disorientatedly. The process is taking a lot out of him. He sees* RAY *relax slightly, and sits down himself. He glances over at* RAY, *goes back to the book he's been reading.*

RAY. What ye readin?

NEIL. Still e same.

RAY. Christ, a five-year-old would've finished it by now.

NEIL. Hey, we're noh all fucking geniuses.

RAY. Read it til me, eh?

NEIL. Read it yursel, yur noh a bairn.

RAY. Chaist read it, eh? Please Neil.

NEIL. Yeah. Okay.

NEIL *settles down to read,* RAY *to listen.*

NEIL. 'She had risen, and now at last a fear assailed him. "What is it?" he cried, shrinking. "I will turn up the light," she said, "And then you can see for yourself". For almost the only time in his life that I know of, Peter was afraid. "Don't turn up the light," he cried. She let her hands play with the hair of the tragic boy. She was not a little girl heartbroken about him; she was a grown woman smiling at it all, but they were wet smiles. Then she turned on the light and Peter saw. He gave a cry of pain; and when the tall beautiful creature stooped to lift him in her arms he drew back sharply. "What is it," he cried again. "I am old Peter. I am ever so much more than twenty. I grew up long ago." "You promised not to." "I couldn't help it Peter. I am a married woman." '

RAY (*whispered*). No you're not.

NEIL. Yes, and the little girl in the bed is my baby.

RAY. No she's not.

NEIL. Ye okay?

RAY. Yeah. Read.

NEIL. It'll be over soon, eh?

RAY. Yeah.

NEIL. 'He took a step towards the sleeping child with his dagger upraised. Of course he didn't strike. He sat down on the floor instead and sobbed; and Wendy did not know how to comfort him, though she could have done it so easily once. She was only a woman now, and she ran out of the room to try to think. Peter continued to cry, and soon his sobs woke Jane. She sat up in bed and was interested at once. "Boy," she said, "Why are you crying?" ' Are ye okay?

RAY *has gotten up off the sofa with a groan and now sits with his head in his hands.*

RAY. I need some stuff Neil.

NEIL. I know. Let it pass.

RAY. Noh. Stuff fie e garage. Should've got it before. Aspirin. Orange Juice. Mars bar or something. Something wi' sugar.

NEIL. Will it be open?

RAY. Yeah. Go will ye. Get me some stuff, it will only take ye ten minutes.

NEIL. Ye be okay on yur own?

RAY. Yeah, please Neil . . . I need it.

NEIL. Okay. (*He stands.*) Ten minutes yeah?

RAY. Thanks.

> RAY *falls back onto the sofa, clutching a pillow or blanket to his chest.* NEIL *watches him, then goes.* RAY *rolls over the sofa and crawls on the floor. He finds* NEIL'*s bag and goes inside it, checking all the pockets, etc. He throws it aside. He sees* NEIL'*s spare jeans sitting out. He grabs for them, goes through the pockets, finds a wrap, falls back smiling, holding the heroin up to the light. He jumps to his feet and starts checking the room for works. None can be seen. He goes to the kitchen and empties out the dustbin. He finds a discarded set of works. He rinses it off in a glass of water, empties the heroin into a spoon, puts in water.*

Shit.

> *He goes back into the rubbish, finds a discarded Jif lemon and squeezes the last drops out of it with an agonising wait for the tiny droplets to fall. He heats the heroin.*

Oh come on, come on motherfucker.

> *He pulls a filter off a cigarette with his teeth, drops in a bit, sucks up the liquid into the syringe.*

Come on, come on, come on.

> *He is strapping a belt onto his arm, frantically slapping for a vein to appear.*

Oh ya cunt . . .

The needle goes in. Instant relief.

Fuck.

Scene Fifteen

NEIL *returns.* RAY *is lying where we left him.*

NEIL. Ye okay? Got yur stuff. Noh aspirins, but I got some paras. Some morning oot ere. Should see it, eh? Ray . . . Ray?

He goes over and looks at him.

Ray . . .

He pulls him up then lets him fall. He turns away, then looks again.

Ray . . . Oh, ya prick . . .

Scene Sixteen

AMANDA *and* CHAIMIG *are taking a gentle stroll.*
AMANDA *has her letter of acceptance in her hand, which she is about to post.* NEIL *sits by the road with his rucksack, trying to hitch a lift.*

CHAIMIG. Far are we now. Are we at at coarner yet?

AMANDA. Aye, chaist aboot. We'll go roond by e post box, okay?

CHAIMIG. Aye, micht as weel. Post at letter of yours. (AMANDA *pauses.*) Fit's at? Fit ye stoppin for?

AMANDA. It's Neil.

CHAIMIG. Fa?

AMANDA. Neil, Ray's pal. He's over by e junction.

CHAIMIG. Neil? Aye. Neil . . . Neil! Neil boy!

NEIL *looks back. He stands and waits for them to come up to him.*

CHAIMIG. Yur still wi' us are ye? A'd've thocht ye'd be pinin for e bricht lichts by now.

NEIL. Noh, a'm still here. Chaist headin off.

CHAIMIG. Yu'll need til take iss ine wi' ye. She's got her hert set on flyin sooth too.

AMANDA. Yur awiy then?

NEIL. Yeah. I'm headin back. Stayed longer than I meant to as it is.

CHAIMIG. Is Raymond noh wi' ye?

NEIL. Ray? Noh . . . Ray's . . . Ray's back at e hoose.

CHAIMIG. Yur noh travellin agither?

AMANDA. Ray's stayin Grandad. D'ye noh mind me tellin ye?

CHAIMIG. Course a mind. A thocht he'd be goin back first, gettin his stuff. She thinks a'm dottled, Neil? D'ye believe at? Thinks cos she's got a couple o 'O' grades she's e sharpest tack in e box.

NEIL. Noh, Ray was gonna come, but he's noh feelin too good. I decided to go on ma own.

AMANDA. Did ye get things sorted?

NEIL. Yeah. We got things sorted.

CHAIMIG. We'll maybe go in and see him. See if he needs anything.

NEIL. He's sleepin now. Ye should leave it a while, eh?

NEIL *starts looking towards the road. He sniffs a bit, wipes his noses, moving from foot to foot.*

CHAIMIG. Yur noh soundin too healthy yursel, Neil. Ye can always stiy wi' us if yur comin doon wi' something.

NEIL. Noh, I'm fine . . . just a bit shivery, at's all . . .

AMANDA. Probably e same thing Ray's got, eh?

NEIL *picks up his bag and puts it on his back.*

NEIL. Yeah. A wouldna be surprised.

AMANDA. C'mon ye. See ye eh?

AMANDA *leads* CHAIMIG *away.* NEIL *turns back towards the road and sticks out his thumb.*

A Nick Hern Book

Among Unbroken Hearts first published in Great Britain in 2001 as an original paperback by Nick Hern Books Limited, 14 Larden Road, London W3 7ST

Among Unbroken Hearts © 2001 by Henry Adam

Henry Adam has asserted his right to be identified as the author of this work

Front cover photograph © Euan Myles

Typeset by Country Setting, Kingsdown, Kent CT14 8ES

Printed and bound in Great Britain by Cox and Wyman

A CIP catalogue record for this book is available from the British Library

ISBN 1-85459 641-1